MW01029715

To:

_____

From:

_____

Date:

_____

God Above All

90 DEVOTIONS TO KNOW THE LIFE-ALTERING LOVE OF GOD

 ZONDERVAN®

ZONDERVAN
God Above All

Copyright © 2020 by Zondervan

Requests for information should be addressed to:

Zondervan, *3900 Sparks Dr. SE, Grand Rapids, Michigan 49546*

ISBN 978-0-310-45535-6 (hardcover)
ISBN 978-0-310-45569-1 (eBook)

Art direction: Sabryna Lugge
Cover Design: Sabryna Lugge
Interior Design: Kristy Edwards
Compiled and written by Steven Watts

Printed in China

20 21 22 23 24   DSC   10 9 8 7 6 5 4 3 2 1

God Above All

WHO ARE WE?

Great are You, O Lord, and greatly to be praised; great is Your power, and infinite is Your wisdom. Man desires to praise You, for he is a part of Your creation; he bears his mortality about with him and carries the evidence of his sin and the proof You resist the proud. Still he desires to praise You, this man who is only a small part of Your creation. You have prompted him that he should delight to praise You, for You have made us for Yourself and our hearts are restless until they find their rest in You.

CONFESSIONS, 1.1.1, TRANS. A. C. OUTLER*.

According to some, we are not much of anything at all. Our lives barely register in the vast history of the universe. Life itself is just one great cosmic accident. There is no greater purpose, no greater truth.

But this isn't God's perspective. Although we are a "small part" of creation, we have a purpose, and this purpose is greater than anything we could possibly imagine. We have been made for God Himself. And our truest innate desire is to praise Him. Nothing less will ever make us truly happy or fully alive.

Yet we have forgotten who we are.

We love, but we do not know the One who is Love. We praise, but we praise what has been made and not the One who has made all things. We are so often in conflict with ourselves and with one another. We are proud when we should be humble.

So we are restless. Restless until we find our rest in Him.

St. Augustine invites you to recover your true identity and find your rest. As you read and reflect on what he has to say, be prepared to meet God. Encounter Him in His glory, grace, and mercy. See the Creator's fingerprints in the world He has made. Offer your brokenness and disordered desires, and receive His healing and care. Follow the path He sets before you. Drink from the fountain of Wisdom, and read from His Word. Let Him transform the way you love yourself and the way you love your community. Love Him. Praise Him. This is who you are.

IN A MOTHER'S ARMS

What praises could we give, what thanks could we offer for God's self-giving love? He, through Whom time was made, loved us so much He was made in time for us. He, older than the world in His eternity, was younger than many of His servants in the world. He, Who had made humanity, became man. He, Who created His mother, was born to her. He formed the hands that carried Him. He filled the breasts that fed Him. The Word, without which human eloquence is rendered mute, wailed—an infant, wordless, in a manger.

SERMON 188, TRANS. S. WATTS.

H ave you ever held a baby in your arms? Felt the warmth of their body? Looked into their eyes when they recognize a familiar voice?

If so, you've probably also heard a baby's ear-splitting wail. You've seen their face, wet with tears and scrunched up in frustration—a frustration you may have shared as you struggled, almost hopelessly, to find a solution.

Augustine, in this Christmas sermon, wasn't being sentimental. A father himself, he was aware of the wonder, challenge, and even heartache these newly formed humans embody the moment their lungs fill with air. Yet that is why he finds Jesus' birth to be a cause for such praise, gratitude, and amazement.

The One who created all things was formed in a womb. His mother bore Him and then held Him in her arms. He cried and she fed Him. And why did He choose to do this? Because He loves us so much. Because He loves *you* so much.

Reflect upon what this passage reveals to you about God's love. Imagine yourself as a child, wrapped up in the comfort of your mother's arms. Imagine staring lovingly into the eyes of your newborn child. Remember that this love does not depend on what you do—only that the One who made you loves you *this much*.

3

NOTHING IS GREATER THAN LOVE

*And now regarding love, which the Apostle says is greater than
the other two—that is, faith and hope—for the more richly
it dwells in a person, the better the person in whom it dwells.
For when we ask whether someone is good, we are not asking
what they believe, or hope, but what they love. Now, beyond all
doubt, the person who loves aright believes and hopes rightly.*

Enchiridion, 31.117, trans. A. C. Outler*.

S erving people can be hard work. Although good in itself, it is often a thankless task. The more you give, the more people ask of you and the more they take. Some are thankful, others not so much. It can be all too easy to grow tired and burnt out.

Augustine wrote this passage after twenty-five years in ministry. Who could blame him if he had started to feel as if he needed a break? Yet when he finally sat down to write about what it means to become a follower of Jesus, his words held no hint of bitterness. Instead, Augustine wrote warmly about one of the Bible's most famous and enduring passages— the apostle Paul's tribute in 1 Corinthians 13 to faith, hope, and, above all, love.

For Augustine—as it was for Paul—love is at the heart of what it means to be a Christian. The more God's love lives in us, the more it will change what we hope for and what we believe. This may mean we no longer fear uncertainty because our hope is now in Jesus. Perhaps we decide to spend our money differently because we believe what we really need is Him.

Receive Augustine's reflection on God's transforming love as both an encouragement and an opportunity. If life is wearing you down, if you find your faith misplaced and your hope faltering, don't try to push through. Instead, reach out to God. Ask Him for the gift of His love. It will restore and transform you.

4

LED TO THE GOOD

We are commanded to love this Good with all our heart, with all our soul, with all our strength. To this Good we ought to be led by those who love us, and to lead those we love. Thus are fulfilled those two commandments on which hang all the Law and the Prophets: "You shall love the Lord your God with all your heart, and with all your mind, and with all your soul;" and "You shall love you neighbor as yourself."

CITY OF GOD, 10.3, TRANS. M. DODS*.

We are usually pretty good at giving recommendations to our friends. We might recommend a favorite restaurant, an interesting book we've read, or a movie we really enjoyed. Sometimes these recommendations work out. Other times, not so much.

The stakes for these kinds of things tend to be pretty low. At worst, the meal might be underwhelming and your friends might be more hesitant to take your advice next time around. But what about matters of much greater significance? Are we as good at recommending a better way of life? Or are we concerned we might overstep? Or our friends will be disappointed or annoyed?

In this passage, Augustine encourages us to love more fully, more courageously, and with greater purpose. Further, when Jesus commands us to love God and our neighbor as ourselves, He sees a community of people encouraging one another to seek not just the good things in life but the Good itself—God Himself. To love our neighbors means both to lead them and to be led by them to God. Then we will all find true happiness together.

Think of the people in your life who love you. Do they lead you to the Good? Do they lead you to God? Are they willing to journey with you, even to be led by you? If not, ask God to bring others into your life who will. Ask Him as well to help you love others in ways that will be purposeful and life changing.

5

TRUE LOVE

For only true love should be called love, otherwise it is lust. And so it is incorrect to say of those who lust that they love, and those who love that they lust. But this is true love, that holding fast to the truth we may live righteously and so despise all mortal things for the sake of the love of people, intending that they live righteously as well.

ON THE TRINITY, 8.7.10, TRANS. A. W. HADDAN*.

W hat is the difference between love and lust? When it comes to romance in popular culture, the difference seems almost nonexistent. In fact, both love and lust end up looking like two kinds of the same desire: to have something or someone. And when desire vanishes? So does love.

This is a confusion Augustine knew only too well. It was as present in his culture as it is in ours. He believed, however, in a meaningful difference between love and lust.

Augustine teaches true love is from God. Love is a gift. It's selfless. It seeks justice. It looks to eternity. Lust, however, is the opposite. It takes. It's selfish. It seeks to dominate. It's concerned only with its needs and wants in the here and now.

Although Augustine is writing about romance in particular, he's *really* concerned with what ultimately motivates us—what we desire. To love is to participate in the Creator's love for creation. To lust is to seek after our own satisfaction.

I encourage you to listen attentively to the world around you. As you encounter the many messages found in popular culture—whether in film, television, music, or on the Internet—ask yourself if the messages ultimately promote selflessness or selfishness, justice or domination, true or false love. Take a moment to consider how different those messages would be if they sought to inspire and encourage true love.

6

TWO SOCIETIES

Two societies have been formed by two loves: the earthly by the love of self, even to the contempt of God; the heavenly by the love of God, even to the contempt of self. The former, in a word, glorifies itself; the latter glorifies the Lord. . . . The one lifts up its head in its own glory; the other says to God, "You are my glory, you lift up my head."

CITY OF GOD, 14.28, TRANS. N. DODS*.

I am sure we have all heard it many times over. Perhaps we have said it too, whether out loud or in the depths of our hearts. *If it makes me happy and doesn't hurt anyone . . .* This justification, or something like it, assumes what we choose to do affects only ourselves. Now, I don't think we actually believe this, which is why we try to justify it in the first place. We just don't want to be held responsible.

Augustine won't let us off the hook so easily. Our desires, our motivations, and our loves are like stones thrown into still water. The ripples go on and on.

For Augustine, our choices ultimately build one of two societies, which, though invisible to the naked eye, are found in every culture. The selfish, who seek their own glory, form one society; the selfless, who glorify God, form the second. And while many may not appear to belong entirely to one society or the other, their choices reveal their true loyalty.

Every decision, then, however insignificant it might seem to you, has a far-reaching impact. But do not feel burdened by the weight of this responsibility. See it instead as an opportunity. When you choose to act selflessly, you participate in a heavenly society. And every little bit helps. Write a list of the ways you can help foster this society—how you might seek the happiness of others as well as your own.

UNTIL THE BITTER END

*For all who love pride and power with empty vanity and the
display of arrogance, and all spirits who desire such things
and seek their own glory by dominating others, are bound
together in one association. . . . And all men and all spirits
who humbly seek the glory of God and not their own, and who
follow Him devoutly, belong to one fellowship. Nevertheless,
God is most merciful and patient with the ungodly, and
offers them an opportunity to repent and be corrected.*

ON THE CATECHIZING OF THE UNINSTRUCTED,
19.31, TRANS, S. D. F. SALMOND*.

H ave you ever found yourself in a conflict without hope of reconciliation? Perhaps someone wronged you, and the person who hurt you was unwilling to ask for forgiveness. Perhaps you were the one at fault and weren't able to swallow your pride.

We have different ways of responding to these situations. Sometimes we lash out and let our anger get the better of us. Sometimes we do everything in our power to make the other person *go away*. Sometimes we do our best to ignore the individual, despite the unresolved conflict lingering in our hearts and minds.

Augustine tells us unresolved conflict lies at the heart of every culture: Those who seek justice often find themselves at odds with those who seek domination. The humble will never find common ground with the proud.

Yet God chooses to be patient even when we are not. Until the bitter end, He gives even His worst enemies an opportunity to change and to be reconciled both to Him and to those whom they have harmed.

If you are like most people, you have unresolved conflict in your life. It might be ever-present, or it might wake you up in the middle of the night without warning. Ask the Lord to take your place in that argument. Give the conflict to Him. Pray He will give you His heart, His patience, and His grace to desire reconciliation—even until the bitter end.

8

THE RIGHT KIND
OF PRIDE

*Humility is especially recommended to the people of the city of
God while they journey in the world. . . . The humble
city is comprised of holy people and good angels, the prideful
city of wicked people and evil angels. The former is guided
and fashioned by the love of God, the latter by the love of self.*

CITY OF GOD, 14.13, TRANS. M. DODS*.

I t is not wrong to take pride in yourself, your community, and your work. Taking pride in these areas shows they are worthy of respect. They are valuable and worth investing in. Further, such pride reflects the dignity our Creator has given to all He has made. This is not the pride Augustine is talking about.

What Augustine is talking about, however, is the pride that refuses to apologize and treats other people as being somehow unworthy of respect. It produces entitlement, a lack of accountability, and an unquenchable thirst for other people's praise. This is the pride that belongs to the city of men. It is disordered and destined for destruction. It is the devil's work—the very same who, as the poet John Milton put it, would rather rule in hell than serve in heaven.

But what are we to do in the face of this pride? Should we fight fire with fire? Treat the prideful with the same lack of respect they show to us? No. Augustine shows us another way—the way of Jesus, the way of the heavenly city.

Contemplate what it means to be truly humble, just as Jesus was truly humble. Remind yourself that this does not mean self-loathing, a willingness to be taken advantage of, or just another opportunity to win approval. It is simply not caring about whether the watching world rightfully praises or wrongly blames you. Ask God to help you realign your priorities. Seek His praise alone. Love others as you love yourself and as God loves you.

9

OUT OF THE MOUTHS OF BABES

"Why not now? Why not put an end to my impure life this very hour?" As I was saying these things and weeping in the bitterest grief of my heart, I suddenly heard the voice of a boy or a girl (I do not know which) coming from the neighboring house, chanting over and over again, "Pick up and read; pick up and read."... Stemming the flood of my tears, I got to my feet, for I understood it to be a divine command to open the Bible and read the first passage I found.

CONFESSIONS, 8.12.28–9, TRANS. A. C. OUTLER*.

I magine knowing your life needed to change, and I mean *really* change. But no matter how hard you tried, no matter how much you wanted to, you simply couldn't find the strength. But maybe you don't need to use your imagination. Maybe this speaks to where you are now. With tears in his eyes, kneeling in a garden in Milan, Augustine is right there with you.

By all appearances, Augustine had it made. From a farmer's son to a professor in a big city, he had succeeded beyond his wildest dreams. On the inside, though, he was deeply unsatisfied. His desires had left him unfulfilled. They had led him to addiction. Nothing he did seemed to make a difference.

But then he heard a voice: God spoke to him, surprisingly, in the words of a child. Humbled and helpless, Augustine listened. What else could he do?

James 4:10 says God lifts up the humble. He did this for Augustine, and He will do it for you. Reflect on the struggles of your heart. Reflect on those battles no one else can see, even the ones you are secretly losing. And for each conflict, speak these truths to God, whether aloud or in the depths of your heart: "You know. You see. Only You can speak peace to the storms that rage inside me."

After saying this prayer, spend some time listening. Listen for God's voice—even in the words of a child.

10

ENJOYING
FORBIDDEN FRUIT

*There was a pear tree near our vineyard. It was heavy with
fruit, whose color and flavor held little appeal. Late one
night—having stayed out playing games in the streets, as
was our bad habit—our group of young troublemakers went
to shake the tree and steal its fruit. We carried off a huge
load, but not to eat ourselves, only to throw to the pigs. In
fact, we barely tasted the fruit. The best part was we knew
we were doing something forbidden. See my heart, O God,
see my heart, which You pitied in the depths of the abyss.*

CONFESSIONS, 2.4.9, TRANS. S. WATTS.

D id you ever do something you almost instantly regretted? Did you choose a harsh word when you could have chosen a kinder one? Did you treat someone poorly, knowing it was wrong at the time, but still somehow enjoying it all the same? What is it about ourselves that chooses to do things we know we shouldn't? Why do we love what we should hate?

Augustine was not afraid to ask himself these hard, uncomfortable questions. This is why he wrote about this episode from his past. He knew he should not have stolen that fruit, but he did it anyway—just for the thrill of it. He knew too that even our smallest decisions, or smallest mistakes, can reveal much deeper truths, truths we would rather not admit to ourselves.

Pray for God to show you the fullness of His compassion. And then, in the knowledge of His grace for you, ask Him to bring to mind those actions and decisions, whether large or small, you wish had never happened. Do not seek to cover them up. Do not try to explain or justify them. Definitely do not try to compensate for them. Pray for and receive His forgiveness. He knows your heart. Although you may feel helpless, He is your help.

11

ONE LAST THING

*"Not in carousing and drunkenness, not in sexual immorality
and debauchery, not in dissension and jealousy. Rather,
clothe yourselves with the Lord Jesus Christ, and do not think
about how to gratify the desires of the flesh." I wanted to read
no further, nor did I need to. For instantly, as the sentence
ended, my heart was infused with something like the light of
full certainty and all the gloom of doubt vanished away.*

CONFESSIONS, 8.12.29, TRANS. A. C. OUTLER*.

A mother and toddler were in the family kitchen. In the toddler's hand was a glass of water. "Honey," the mother said, "you need to give that to me." The toddler gripped the glass more firmly and said, "No." This was a standoff. The mother, like any parent, wanted her child to be safe. But just as importantly, she wanted her child to trust her. A toddler with a glass full of water was hardly a recipe for success.

Thank goodness parents are not like their children! Thank goodness adults are willing to hand over everything to their Father, trusting He has their best interests in mind. Well, except for that . . . *one last thing*. The older we get, the better we get at making excuses: "I deserve it" or "It's not that big of a deal anyway." But of course, if that were true, we would have let go long ago.

Augustine, at the very point of giving his life to God, found it difficult to give everything over. He increasingly liked the idea of Christianity, but he kept holding on to that *one last thing*. And in doing so, he didn't really give up anything. For Augustine, it was the satisfaction he found in sexual desire. "Give me chastity," he once said, "but not yet!"

Augustine finally received peace when he finally let go.

What is that glass of water in your life? Is it a dream job or dream home? Is it your parents' approval? None of these things are necessarily bad—some of them can be very good. But would you be willing to listen to God if He asked you to let them go? Trust Him, and then let go.

12

RECALL TO MIND

I want to bring to mind my past wickedness and the carnal corruptions of my soul—not because I still love them, but that I may love You, O God. I do this for the love of Your love, recalling in the bitterness of self-examination my wicked ways, that You may grow sweet to me, Your sweetness without deception, happy and assured. You gathered me up out of those pieces into which I had been torn, for I had turned away from the Oneness of You, and lost myself among "the many."

CONFESSIONS, 2.1.1, TRANS. A. C. OUTLER*.

I n the world of professional sports, having a short memory is probably helpful. Dwelling on yesterday's failures or successes won't get you the next victory.

In the spiritual life, however, this philosophy can lead to trouble. In choosing to leave the past behind completely, we can take God for granted. We can convince ourselves our progress is due to our abilities, not His grace and provision. We can also too easily forget those who loved and helped us along the way in our times of need.

When Augustine talks about his past, he isn't interested in championing his spiritual journey. He is not even concerned with keeping himself humble. As far as Augustine is concerned, God was, and remains, the hero of his story. In recalling his earlier misdeeds, Augustine remembers the love God once showed and continues to show him.

Reflect back on the past few years. When did you feel most in need? When did you feel most broken, in desperate need of being put back together? If you have a pen and paper at hand, write these moments down on the left side of the page. When you finish, look back over the list. Did God meet those needs? If so, write those blessings on the opposite side of the page. May these blessings help you remember just how good God is to you, how He has restored you, and how He will continue to carry you, whether you're broken or whole.

GIVEN MORE

The Lord says, "Whoever has will be given more." He will give, then, to those who have. This means if people freely and cheerfully use what He has given to them, He will add to and perfect His gifts. The loaves in the miracle numbered only five and seven before they were divided among the hungry. But once they were distributed, and many thousands were fed, baskets were filled with the leftovers. Now, just as that bread increased in the very act of breaking it, so the Lord will multiply, by His grace, the thoughts He has already given me for this task as soon as I begin to offer them to others.

ON CHRISTIAN TEACHING, 1.1.1, TRANS. J. SHAW*.

W hoever has will be given more" (Matthew 13:12). In a society driven by an unrelenting desire for more of everything, Jesus' statement might appear to strike a false note. Hasn't this led to income inequality, unhealthy diets, and the misuse of creation? Or perhaps His words might be an affirmation: material possessions are the result of God's blessing. Well, aren't they? Sometimes, yes; sometimes, no. In the Old Testament, some of Israel's richest kings were furthest from God's heart. *More* does not necessarily mean *more of God*.

Augustine reads these words of Jesus in a different light. He understands them as an expression of God's ongoing, unrivaled generosity. God gives so we may give. And when we give, He loves to give us more. The last thing we should do is store up for ourselves. That would defeat the purpose. This would amount to loving the *more*, when that *more* should bless those whom God loves.

Augustine hopes God will do the same for his work as Jesus did for the loaves and fishes. May we share the same hope.

Reflect on all you have received from God. How can you share with those in need? Pray for God to take your talents or your resources and make them *more*. Lastly, find a practical way to put that prayer into action. Where is there a need? How can you be generous to others as God has been generous to you?

14

DON'T TAKE YOUR GOODNESS FOR GRANTED

Grace is from the One who calls. The good works that result, however, are from the one who receives that grace. Good works, then, do not produce grace, but are produced by grace. . . . No one, therefore, does good works in order to receive grace, but because they have received it. . . . Grace comes first; good works come second.

TO SIMPLICIANUS, TRANS. S. WATTS.

G etting to know at-risk youths can be a shock to the system. But it isn't the substance abuse, absent parents, or petty crime that is most disturbing. It is the slow realization that whatever you had previously thought made you "better" than the kids you are spending time with is often little credit to yourself. Sure, you may work hard—and life is rarely easy for anyone—but if you had grown up in a similar situation, it could just as easily be you who was considered at-risk.

Augustine knew just how little credit he deserved for his goodness. In fact, he believed he wasn't capable of goodness at all if not for God's grace. After all, if not for God's gift of life, would any of us be alive? Goodness, like life itself, is a gift. Don't take it for granted.

Thank God we cannot earn His grace, no matter how hard we try. Thank God He is not quicker to give or forgive because of our accomplishments or mistakes. May we have the humility to know our goodness does not make us better than His other children.

Let your goodness grow in gratitude instead. Let your heart be warmed to others who are just as much in need of His generosity as you are. May it transform the way you love the unloved.

15

BECOMING MORE
DEPENDENT

We work, too, of course; but we are fellow-workers with God who does the work, because His mercy goes before us. He goes before us, however, so that we may be healed; but then He also follows us, so that by being healed we may grow healthy and strong. He goes before us that we may be called; He will follow us that we may be glorified. He goes before us so that we might lead devout lives; He will follow us so that we may always live with Him, because without Him we can do nothing.

ON NATURE AND GRACE, 35, TRANS. P. HOLMES AND R. E. WALLIS*.

One of the goals of parenting is to prepare your children for the world. One day they will grow up and, hopefully, leave the house. The idea is they will become increasingly independent, even self-sufficient. They'll earn a living, find a home, and maybe start a family of their own.

While we often talk of God as our Father and ourselves as His children, Augustine reminds us our relationship with God doesn't quite work in the same way. God doesn't watch us grow up in the expectation He'll be able to send us into the world as self-sufficient adults. Independence is not the goal. It was never His goal.

God heals us to strengthen us, not that we might become self-sufficient, but that we might know Him and depend upon Him fully. He is before us, He is beside us, and He follows after us. And when we work, we work with Him.

Spend some time in prayer. Ask God to show you how you might depend upon Him fully. Reflect on the choices you made over the past week. Did these contribute to a greater sense of independence *from* God or dependence *upon* Him? If you need His healing, ask Him to heal you. If you are weak, ask for His strength. Pray that, in the upcoming week, He will invite you to participate in the work He is already doing all around you.

16

BE GOD'S MERCY

*Scripture says both: The God of my mercy shall go before
me, and again this: Your mercy shall follow me all the
days of my life. Let us then reveal our life to Him by
confession, not praise our life by defending it. For if it is
not His way but our own, it cannot be the right way.*

ON NATURE AND GRACE, 35, TRANS. P. HOLMES AND R. E. WALLIS*.

F ormal evaluations are rarely pleasant experiences. Whether at work or school, they often produce a distinct feeling of dread in the pits of our stomachs. Even for the most confident among us, the worry still lingers that maybe the evaluation won't work out as expected. We become defensive, and we often fear the worst.

Some of us think of God in similar terms. We believe He is always evaluating us, always testing us. And when He sees our lives, we hope He doesn't look too closely. Sometimes we almost prefer He doesn't look at all. At least then we won't feel so *judged*.

Augustine doesn't have any illusions about our standing before a perfect, holy God. We can't just pretend we aren't sinners in need of His grace. But Augustine makes it clear when God looks upon us and upon the messiness of our lives, He doesn't do so as a judge who is itching to show us where we've come up short, itching to condemn us.

His mercy goes before us. It follows behind us. It surrounds us.

Pray you become more aware of God's mercy. Pray you know in your heart of hearts you do not need to explain yourself to Him. You don't need to be defensive. You are not on trial.

Consider some ways you can show God's mercy to others. Perhaps these individuals also try to keep God at arm's length, fearful of what He might think of them. Perhaps they are tired of going their own way. Be God's mercy to them.

17

THE FREEDOM
TO CHOOSE

*[Free will] faithfully prays and says: "Direct my footsteps
according to Your word; let no sin rule over me." . . . It
prays, it does not promise; it confesses, it does not claim.
It seeks the greatest freedom, it does not boast of its own
power . . . The freedom of the will is not annihilated by
being helped; it is helped because it is not annihilated. The
person who says to God, "Be my Helper," confesses they want
to do what they have been commanded, but asks help from
the One who gave the order so it may be carried out.*

LETTER 157, TRANS. S. WATTS.

Western society puts a premium on freedom of choice. We want to be able to decide whom we love, what we buy, and for whom we vote. In fact, we consider it our right. And why shouldn't we have our say and follow our hearts and minds, rather than someone else's?

Unfortunately, we are rarely as free as we think we are. Our options are often limited. We often do not receive all the necessary information, and what we know may well be wrong. We have the freedom to vote, for instance, but that doesn't mean the candidates are any good. Our freedom to choose, if we choose poorly, could lead to a loss of freedom.

Augustine offers a different perspective. He argues freedom isn't really about our being able to choose one thing over another. Instead, we find true freedom only in God because only God is truly free. Rather than make our own choices, then, we should seek His advice.

It may seem strange to say it, but one finds freedom in giving up control. Freedom comes from trusting God's Word, trusting His faithfulness, and receiving His help. If you are struggling with a big decision, if you feel weighed down by many burdens, seek the Lord's freedom. He will be your help.

THE JOURNEY

Suppose, then, we are travelers in a foreign country who could not live happily while away from our homeland. . . . Wishing to put an end to our misery, we choose to return home. We find, however, we must make use of some mode of travel, either by land or water, in order to get home—the place where we are truly happy. But the beauty of the country through which we pass, and the pleasure of the journey itself, charm our hearts. And so we enjoy what we should otherwise use to get to our destination, no longer being in a hurry to get there. We have become entertained by false enjoyment, diverted from the home whose delights would make us truly happy.

ON CHRISTIAN TEACHING, 1.4.4, TRANS. J. SHAW*.

W hat really makes you happy? What do you really want? What are the goals, beyond anything else, you really want to accomplish?

These are important questions to ask ourselves. In truth, we probably don't ask them enough. Life has so many day-to-day obligations, let alone emergencies, we easily lose sight of what we value most.

Often, we find ourselves making do with a kind of second-rate happiness. This might be something good on its own terms, but this lesser happiness ultimately distracts us from what really matters. For instance, completing that last work project might give you a better start for the upcoming day, but its value pales in comparison to spending quality time with family or friends.

One of Augustine's biggest concerns is losing sight of what really makes us happy. He distinguishes between what we enjoy—what makes us happy—and what we use to seek that enjoyment. Unfortunately, so many of us get distracted on the way to our ultimate destination. Instead of pressing on toward our true goal, we find ourselves making do with second best.

Write down, or say aloud, the answers to the questions we started with. If, like Augustine's traveler, you find yourself distracted from your goals, ask yourself why. What in your life brings you second-rate happiness? How do they prevent you from arriving at your true destination? Is your true happiness found in God, or do you need to reorient your journey?

19

A NEW EXERCISE
REGIMEN

*The mind must be purified so it can perceive that light,
and cling to it. . . . Let us look upon this purification as
a kind of journey or voyage to our homeland. For it is
not by moving from one place to another that we come
nearer to God, who is everywhere, but by the cultivation
of pure desires and virtuous habits. But we should have
been wholly incapable of this, had not Wisdom come
down to adapt Himself to our weakness, and to show us a
pattern of holy life in the form of our own humanity.*

ON CHRISTIAN TEACHING, 1.10.10–11, TRANS. J. SHAW*.

N o one said exercise is easy. Your body aches, your lungs burn, and your heart beats loudly in your chest. And to make exercise worthwhile, you can't only exercise once in a while. It has to become part of your life's rhythm. You have to exercise even when you don't want to.

What is true of the body is also true of the mind. We know sitting around all day and eating junk food is unhealthy. But so is being lazy in our thinking and getting stuck in bad mental habits. Shouldn't we be seeking after the truth and growing in wisdom, even if, like exercise, doing so takes work?

Augustine believes our minds need training, just like our bodies. But this isn't really about getting smarter or reading more books. It is ultimately about pursuing Wisdom, which, for Augustine, is another way of talking about God. As we train, as we purify our minds, we receive more of His knowledge, more of His light. And we illustrate this knowledge and light by the choices we make day to day.

We can do this, Augustine encourages us, because God shows us the way. We can see our progress, then, by looking at His example—Jesus.

Plan out an exercise regime for your mind. What steps can you take to improve your mental diet? What needs to be cut out? What needs to be improved? Remember, just like training the body, this exercise regime for your mind requires work and discipline. It is more than worth the effort!

20

REMEMBER WHEN?

And what tongue can tell, or what imagination can conceive,
the reward He will give at the end. . . . For our comfort
on this earthly journey He has given us so freely of His
Spirit, that in the adversities of this life we may retain our
confidence in, and love for, the One whom we do not yet see.

ON CHRISTIAN TEACHING, 1.15.14, TRANS. J. SHAW*.

I *s it really worth it? Does it really have to be this hard?* How often do questions like these come to mind? And even when you receive help or some much-needed encouragement, you can still barely keep your head above water. Sure, you are no longer drowning, but you don't feel that much closer to land.

Augustine reminds you: Don't forget why you do what you do. It may be difficult to see now, but soon everything will become clear. Remember those times when your hope nearly ran out, but God found a way? They are only the smallest signs of what is to come.

Our journey is long, and often difficult. But if God is our destination, He will give us what we need to carry on. But like so much of what He does, from the greatest to the smallest miracle, this provision is for much more than our present need. Each grace, each encouragement, is also a promise that will be fulfilled at our destination. *It will be worth it.*

Think back over the past year. Reflect on those times when someone offered help or something came through at the very moment when you were most in need. What do these times say about God? What do they reveal in part, of what will be revealed in full, when you finally see Him face-to-face? May you find Him to be a source of great confidence and delight even in the midst of your hardest and darkest days.

21

THE FLESH IS SO WEAK

O Lord my God, my one hope, hear me, lest through weariness I do not wish to seek You, but may always ardently seek Your face. Give me strength to seek, You who has made me find You, and has given me the hope of finding You more and more.

THE TRINITY, 15.28.51, TRANS. A. W. HADDAN*.

In the Garden of Gethsemane, Jesus told His disciples to watch and pray. He came back to find the disciples sleeping. They couldn't even help Jesus in His darkest hour. Then Jesus said these famous words: "The spirit is willing, but the flesh is weak" (Matthew 26:41).

And for us, sometimes the spirit isn't all that willing to begin with. The journey of faith can be tiring for the body and soul. If we think otherwise, we probably didn't pay close enough attention to what Jesus and His disciples endured. We should expect trouble. But God never expected us to face our troubles alone.

Augustine knows we can get worn down. He knows keeping our heads up and our eyes lifted toward our destination is hard. Sometimes just *wanting* to keep going is hard. That is why he prays, "My God, my one hope."

God reveals Himself to you time and time again. He will not abandon you. He will give you strength. He will give you hope. He will offer more and more of Himself as you seek Him more and more.

Make Augustine's prayer your own. No matter where you find yourself at the moment, let this prayer encourage you along your way. Have faith the One who first called you will also give you what you need to continue on. Remember too, no matter how things are: resist the temptation just to simply put your head down and soldier on—choose to bow your head in prayer instead.

IN A RUT

Doesn't it often happen when we show certain spacious and beautiful places, either in the city or in the countryside, to someone who has never seen them—places we tend to pass by without any sense of enjoyment, simply because we have become so used to them—that we find our own enjoyment renewed in their delight as they take in something new? And so our enjoyment increases as our friendship deepens; for as we grow closer and closer in this bond of love, what seemed old becomes new to us again.

On the Catechizing of the Uninstructed, 12.17, trans. S. D. F. Salmond*.

I t's funny how little some things change. Even though he wrote this hundreds of years ago, Augustine described a truth many of us know well today.

If we live somewhere long enough, we often begin to take our surroundings for granted. Perhaps we become too busy to pay attention. Perhaps we fall into a rhythm of life that makes it easy to ignore what's going on beyond our immediate concerns.

But then a friend or family member arrives in town. We show them the sights, our favorite places to eat, and it is like we experience it all for the first time again. Our appreciation is revitalized.

In the Christian life, we have a tendency to take our faith for granted. Maybe our lives are hectic, maybe reading the Bible becomes a tiring obligation, or maybe we lose the spark that first got us on the journey of faith.

Augustine offers this encouragement to anyone who takes his or her faith for granted: *Invite others along on your journey.* In sharing your experiences and your beliefs, you not only include others in your faith, you also help revitalize it.

Do you feel stuck in a rut? Has your faith lost its excitement, its sense of wonder? Perhaps you simply think you could benefit from a different perspective. Think of someone, or perhaps a few people, you would like to invite along for the ride. These might already be friends for whom faith does not play a large role in their lives. Take the opportunity to deepen that relationship through shared commitment.

I AM FEARFULLY AND
WONDERFULLY MADE

If a human artist, who has for some reason made a deformed statue, is able to recast it and make it very beautiful without losing any of the material . . . surely the almighty Artist is capable of doing the same. Can He not remove and eliminate every deformity of the human body, whether common or rare, which, though in keeping with the miseries of life, do not belong to the future happiness of those in heaven?

CITY OF GOD, 22.19, TRANS. M. DODS*.

Our bodies are truly remarkable. So much has to go right for them to function properly—let alone work as well as they do most of the time. Our bodies are really nothing short of a miracle. Yet how often do we take our bodies for granted—that is, of course, until something goes wrong? Age and injury have a way of deepening our appreciation for a fully functioning body. So too do congenital disease, birth defects, and cancer, especially in the young. These can produce a deep sense of injustice, even anger. How could God allow the birth of such a suffering body?

Augustine knew this heartache well. He once was attracted to the idea that our broken, decaying bodies were the problem. True freedom meant an escape from the body's cage. But the Christian story changed his perspective.

Our bodies are wonderfully designed. But their blessings and curses are also signs of deeper spiritual realities. At their best, our bodies point to the goodness of our Creator and His promise to make all things new. At their worst, they represent our spiritual brokenness and separation from our Maker.

Does Augustine's perspective on the body change your own? What does it say about God as an Artist? What does it say about your body in its strength and weaknesses? Read those passages in the Bible (Matthew 9:1–8; Mark 5:21–43; Luke 7:11–17) where Jesus—God among us—healed broken bodies. Reflect on what these healings say about God's compassion for those whose bodies suffer.

24

ELEVATED IN CREATION

Consider the human body. Though it dies like the body of an animal, and is in many ways weaker, it is a revelation of the goodness of God and the providence of the great Creator! . . . Think of the marvelous dexterity which God has given to the tongue and the hands, enabling them to speak and write, and to perform and practice so many tasks and arts.

CITY OF GOD, 22.24, TRANS. M. DODS*.

A *ren't we just animals, anyway?* Augustine acknowledges that, in many respects, this appears to be the case. Like any animal, our bodies suffer, break down, and die. Science shows us we also share many of the same instincts and urges as animals. We even share some DNA.

This acknowledgment has its benefits. It encourages us to treat the rest of creation with greater care and compassion. But this knowledge also has drawbacks. As a result, we might be blind to the extraordinary gulf that separates human beings from the rest of the animal world. For every monkey that uses a rock to crack a nut, a human being performs laser surgery, composes a concerto, or lands a jet on an aircraft carrier.

Augustine has no interest in treating God's other creatures with contempt. But as he looks upon the human body, he sees evidence of the Creator's special design. He sees this especially in the alignment of a person's mental, spiritual, and physical characteristics. Above all creatures, humans have the capacity to be endlessly creative, putting our hopes and beliefs into words and actions in ways that are unparalleled in the rest of the created world.

Faith can sometimes overstress the spiritual at the expense of the physical. As Augustine reminds us, God clearly cares about both because He created both. Reflect on how you can use your body as something created for a greater purpose. This is an affirmation and an opportunity—not a guilt trip. How can the works of your hands and words of your mouth honor their Creator in all of their creativity?

THE BEAUTIES
OF CREATION

*What can I say about the rest of creation, with all its beauty
and usefulness, which God has given to human beings to
behold and serve their purposes, judged and hurled into
the labors and miseries of life as they are? Shall I speak of
the many and various beauties of the sky, earth, and sea?*

CITY OF GOD, 22.24, TRANS. M. DODS*.

D ay to day, we walk out the front door to the car, to the bus, or to the subway station. From there we commute to work and back again. Or perhaps we stay at home, only going out for an appointment or errand. Our world often becomes so small. Our attention focuses on little more than the task at hand. And God can seem just as small, seemingly bound to our own limited horizons.

Sometimes we need to remember to look up and around us. As Augustine reminds us, the world is an astonishing place, full of stunning, beautiful, and breathtaking complexity. Just to be able to appreciate creation is a gift. The world is no cosmic accident. The world is the beloved creation of a good Creator, for both our use and our profound appreciation.

Augustine encourages us not to lose sight of the world around us. When we take in its grandeur, we receive a deeper understanding of God's character and the future He has in store for those who remain faithful until the end. If He did all this for a world still wracked by suffering and death, how much more can we expect of a world filled with heaven's glory?

Take the opportunity this week to look up where you would ordinarily look down. Give yourself time to take the scenic route to work. Practice patience. Pay closer attention. Thank God not only for the wonderful world in which you live, but also for the ability to appreciate it. Thank Him for the gift of sight, sound, taste, touch, and smell.

26

PRAISE THE CREATOR

Let my soul praise You that it may love You. Let it confess Your mercies to You that it may praise You. Your whole creation never ceases nor is silent in Your praises. Every soul praises You, their voice directed towards You. Animals and other physical things praise You through the voices of those who meditate upon them. Our souls, from their weariness, may rise towards You, leaning on those things which You have made, and passing on to You, the One who has wonderfully made them. There, in that place, is refreshment and true strength.

CONFESSIONS, 5.1.1, TRANS. J. G. PILKINGTON*.

D id you ever wonder how a Christian ought to think about creation? Is there an especially *Christian* way to relate to creation?

Genesis 1 tells us when God created the world and everything in it, He saw that it was good. We also know from the Scriptures that God is not to be identified *with* creation. We should not worship what God created (Romans 1:25), whether that is another human being or anything else in the world. We should worship the Creator instead.

Our relationship to creation is not a one-way street. It is not something to be used for whatever we desire. Rather, humans have a responsibility to give voice to the praises of an otherwise inarticulate world. For in contemplating the beauty of a bird's plumage or the radiance of a sunrise, we glorify God on behalf of His creation.

But that is not all. In glorifying God's work in creation, we draw closer to Him. This act uplifts our weary souls and restores them.

Think about your relationship to God's creation. How can you glorify God in the way you think about it, the way you see it, and the way you use it? The next time you go outside or look out the window, find reasons to thank God and to worship Him as the Creator. In praising Him through His creation, may your soul be inspired and renewed.

27

WRESTLING WITH
THE BIBLE

*Whoever, then, thinks they understand the Holy
Scriptures, or any part of them, but interprets them in a
way that does not build up this twofold love of God and
neighbor, does not yet understand them as they should.*

ON CHRISTIAN TEACHING, 1.36.40, TRANS. J. SHAW*.

Have you ever been hurt by the Bible? Was it ever used for an argument you couldn't ever imagine Jesus making? Or maybe the Bible's been used simply as a book of rules, mostly concerned with what you shouldn't do and how bad you are for falling short?

Augustine spent a lot of time reading and *wrestling* with the Bible. As a young man, he found it embarrassing. Later on, he struggled to reconcile some of the stories the Bible told him about God. Over time, and with more than a little help, the Bible became so much more than words on a page. But Augustine didn't keep it all to himself. He wrote a guide for those who wished to understand the Bible better.

Jesus gave us the two greatest commandments: to love God and to love our neighbors as ourselves (Matthew 22:34–40). As far as Augustine was concerned, this is why we read the Bible. Not to win an argument. Not to impress people. Not to have an answer for everything. And certainly not to make God think more highly of us. Rather we read the Bible to grow in our love for God, our neighbors, and ourselves. If that isn't happening, we aren't reading it correctly.

Now, this is much easier in theory than in practice. So let's practice. If you have a Bible at hand, open it. Find a passage, perhaps one that bothers you or one that someone once used to wound you. Or just read the first passage to catch your eye. Before you read, pray: "God, as I read, grow my love for You, for myself, and for my neighbor." May He give you His eyes to see, His ears to hear, and His heart to love.

28

ANTONY'S EXAMPLE

I had heard how Antony, accidentally coming into church while the Gospel was being read, had been admonished as if the reading had been addressed to him: "Go, sell your possessions and give it to the poor, and you will have treasure in heaven. Then come, and follow Me." By such a revelation he was at once converted to You.

And so I quickly returned to the place where Alypius was sitting, for that is where I had put down the Apostle's book when I had gotten up. I snatched it up, opened it, and in silence read the first passage my eyes fell upon.

CONFESSIONS, 5.1.1, TRANS. A. C. OUTLER*.

It really speaks to me. Art, books, music, even movies or television shows—sometimes they just speak to us. We don't know how, but sometimes they peer into the depths of our hearts and understand our circumstances completely. The experience may be fleeting, but it is still important. Perhaps we have even been changed as a result.

Now, who was Antony? He was an Egyptian peasant who lived several generations before Augustine. One day, while thinking about how Jesus' first followers left everything for His sake, Antony entered a church where he heard the gospel of Matthew being read: "Go, sell your possessions . . ." (Matthew 19:21). Believing the message to be directed at him, Antony went and sold everything he owned. Shortly afterward, he entered the desert to be a monk. In the following years his reputation for holiness and miracle-working spread far and wide. His example inspired thousands, Augustine included.

The Word of God spoke and Antony listened. Augustine listened too. Their lives were never the same.

Human hands wrote the Bible, but it speaks with God's voice. Maybe we don't always listen. Perhaps we think a message is for someone else. But let us read the Bible with not just our eyes open, but also our ears—and certainly our hearts. What we hear may well speak to us in ways we haven't been spoken to before. It may just change our lives.

THE WORD OF
GOD IS ALIVE

*The Gospel and living Word of God, which enters into the
marrow of the soul and examines the turning point of the heart,
is offered to us all for our benefit. Its gentle touch only comforts
those who comfort others. Look, the Gospel is presented to us as
a mirror in which we can see ourselves. If we happen to see that
our faces are dirty, we can carefully wipe them clean. That way
we won't be embarrassed the next time we look in the mirror.*

SERMON 301A, TRANS. S. WATTS.

T he Bible really is amazing. It's been printed so many times and found in so many places we can lose sight of just how remarkable it is. Depending on your tradition, it comprises somewhere between sixty-six and eighty-one books. Its pages are filled with great love stories, the rise and fall of kings and queens, hard-fought battles, visionary prophecies, stunning miracles, and even the creation of the world. The Bible also contains four biographies of Jesus, who is without question the most influential person ever to walk the earth.

But while the Bible contains all these stories from long, long ago, Augustine tells us its words do not lie dead and dusty on the page. They are alive. The Author, who stands behind the human authors of its many stories, still breathes life through its pages.

Augustine explains when we read or listen to the Word of God, it is not so much what we do, but what the Word does to us. The Bible works its way into the heart and soul, comforts those who comfort others, shows us our true selves, and then removes our shame.

If you have a Bible at hand, read Matthew 5:1–12. As you read over Jesus' challenging and inspiring words, don't think so much about what you can take from the passage, but what the passage does within you. What do the words do to your heart, to your mind, and to your spirit? Does the passage bring you comfort? Take your shame away? Breathe life into old bones?

30

SAVOR THE WORD

In expounding the Holy Scriptures to you, it is as if I am breaking open bread for you. You, who are hungry, receive it. Burp praises out of the fullness of your heart! You, who have a feast before you, do not be stingy in good works and deeds. What I provide for you does not belong to me. What you eat, I eat; what you live on, I live on. We have in heaven a common storehouse—from it comes the Word of God.

Sermon 45, trans. R. G. MacMullen*.

On certain occasions fast food is exactly what we need. We may be in a rush, on a road trip, or just too tired to cook a meal. But nobody—well nobody but young children—thinks we can live on it. We know the value of sitting down together and enjoying a prepared meal. Doing so is usually healthier, definitely slower, and certainly better for our relationships.

Did you ever think reading or listening to the Bible could be like having a meal? Augustine certainly thought so. But this wasn't fast food. It was a sit-down affair. Augustine, when he preached, broke the bread of the Scriptures. His audiences ate their fill. The words were to be savored and enjoyed together. They were to produce good works—even burps of praise!

Sit down and enjoy a meal with the Scriptures. Even better, invite others to join you in the feast. Choose a psalm, perhaps one of the shorter ones to start. You don't want to overstuff yourself. Maybe choose an old standby, such as Psalm 23. Or maybe Psalm 70—a favorite "recipe" for some of the earliest Christian monks. When you read, read slowly. Savor the words. Chew thoughtfully. Expect God to nourish you, even surprise you!

BIND US TOGETHER

For we are all His temple, each of us individually and all of us together, because He comes down to inhabit each person as well as the whole body in harmony, being no greater in each than in all, since He is neither expanded nor divided. Our heart when it rises to Him is His altar; the priest who intercedes for us is His Only-begotten Son.

CITY OF GOD, 10.3, TRANS. M. DODS*.

W hen a family prepares to welcome a new baby, the checklist can be sizable. Everything from a hospital bag to a car seat needs to be accounted for. But amongst all the practical details, one can't forget that *other* checklist: the emotional one. The other children in the family, especially if they are still young, will often need reassuring. Things are about to change, but having more children does not mean less love for the others.

In ancient Israel, God's presence filled the temple in Jerusalem. But as Augustine explains, followers of Jesus experience that same presence in a different way. Each follower becomes a temple, a place where God dwells. And what's more, the whole community of followers, wherever they are, are *also* God's temple.

This means God's presence is not just with that other person over *there*. He is within you both, equally and together. Whatever your differences and disagreements, the same God is present in equal measure. And not only that, but the same Son works on your behalf, reconciling you to the Father, and reconciling you to one another.

Do you need a reminder that God dwells within you? Maybe you need a reminder that the other follower of Christ with whom you are in conflict is also a temple of the living God. Jesus works within this person as He works within you; His presence binds you together even when you don't get along. May God make His presence known.

32

TRUE FRIENDSHIP

When I first began to teach in my hometown, I had gained a very dear friend, about my own age. . . . We knew each other from childhood and we had both gone to school and played together. But he was not then my friend, nor indeed ever became my friend, in the true sense of the term; for there is no true friendship except between those You bind together and who are joined fast to You by that love which is "poured out into our hearts through the Holy Spirit, who has been given to us."

CONFESSIONS, 4.4.7, TRANS. A. C. OUTLER*.

T rue friendship is a gift. Few things are more important than having someone to call and lean on during trying times. Not all friendships are like this, of course. Some fail under pressure, some rarely deepen beyond surface-level pleasantries. But most know the difference between these kinds of friendships and the ones that last.

Augustine takes our understanding of true friendship, that rare and valuable gift, and deepens it. True friendship, in his view, is shared by those united in their commitment to Jesus. A true friend encourages, loves, and holds the other accountable on the journey to Him. Augustine, for his part, isn't satisfied with simply having another Christian friend if that friendship doesn't center on Christ.

Perhaps this hits a raw nerve. Perhaps your heart aches from a lack of true friendship in your life. May God in His mercy provide you with a worthy companion for the journey. Maybe you have friends, even very good ones, but faith plays only a minor role in the relationships. May God enrich these friendships with His wise and loving presence. And if you have this special kind of Christian friendship, thank God for this rare blessing. May you treasure it the rest of your days.

33

HE'S THERE IN
YOUR LOSS

*As the day now approached on which she was to depart
this life—a day which You knew, but which we did
not—it happened . . . that she and I stood alone,
leaning out of a certain window from which the garden
of the house we occupied in Ostia could be seen. Here,
removed from the crowd, we were resting ourselves
for the voyage after the fatigues of a long journey. We
were talking alone, very pleasantly, "forgetting what
is behind and straining toward what is ahead."*

CONFESSIONS, 9.10.23, TRANS. A. C. OUTLER*.

M any years ago, a daughter, now grown up, looked out her window. Her aged father had just passed and grief took its toll. But as she reflected on the moments they had shared together while he was alive, she noticed something, something unexpected. A blue jay in the yard. No one ever saw blue jays in that part of the world.

They were her dad's favorite bird. She knew, somehow, this was God's doing. He had been there in the love she and her father shared. And He was there now—with her.

Augustine describes a similar kind of story. This one, however, involves a son and his mother. Augustine loved his mother, Monica. He had certainly put her through a lot. But she had remained faithful—faithful to pray, faithful to support him. And soon after Augustine returned to his mother's faith, they shared a beautiful moment together, not knowing it would be one of their last. As they talked, awaiting their voyage back to Africa, God revealed Himself to them in a glorious vision. Augustine never forgot it.

Losing a loved one can feel almost unbearable, as if a part of ourselves has been torn away. Where is God in our loss? Did He depart as well? If you have ever felt this way, or if you feel this way now, be encouraged. God is there in your love for those you have lost. He is there *in* your loss. May He show you how He was present in the love you shared. May He show you He is present still.

IN MY ABSENCE

I beg you, my friends, and implore you, for Christ's sake, not to let my bodily absence grieve you. For I am certain you know I could never be separated in spirit and in deepest love from you. Though perhaps I grieve more than you, because my weakness prevents me from bearing all the cares that have been laid upon me by those members of Christ to whom I must be devoted on account of my fear and love of Him.

LETTER 122, TRANS. J. G. CUNNINGHAM*.

They are with us in spirit. We say it when someone dies, or when someone important to the community moves on. We use it to affirm who they were and what they used to do. Sometimes, however, we mean more than this. We mean somehow, mysteriously, we can feel their presence even if we know they aren't around.

Augustine had to take a leave of absence from his community. He struggled with ill health and couldn't fulfill his obligations. Yet he wanted to remind them even though he couldn't be there in body, he was still there in spirit and in love.

He also wanted them to remain faithful to him, even in his absence. Later in the letter, for instance, Augustine reminded them to continue clothing the poor. They did this when he was among them; they shouldn't stop just because he was no longer there.

It is not unusual to speak a certain way when someone is present, only to behave in a completely different way when he or she is not. Augustine shows us, however, this cannot be the case for true followers of Jesus.

And for yourself, how do you want to be spoken about when you are absent? Are you faithful to do the same when another leaves the room? Feel free to write your answers down. Ask God, in His grace, to unite your community when you are together, and especially when you are apart.

35

BREAKING BAD HABITS

"The flesh lusts against the spirit and the spirit against the flesh." The spirit struggles, not in hatred, but for mastery, because it wants the body, which it loves, to be subject to a higher principle. The flesh struggles, too, not in hatred, but because of the bondage of habit which it has received from its first parents and which has since become ingrained. The spirit, then, in subduing the flesh, works as it were to destroy the ill-founded peace of an evil habit and bring about the real peace, which springs from a good habit.

ON CHRISTIAN TEACHING, 1.24.25, TRANS. J. SHAW*.

B ad habits. Maybe they aren't that big a deal. Or at least you don't think so—although your spouse, friend, or family member may disagree! But perhaps they are a big deal. Every time you behave *that* way, you want to hang your head in shame and desperately try not to do it again. But that's the thing with habits. Good or bad, they are very difficult to break.

Augustine writes here about a bad habit that affects everyone. One that seems so hard to break, it is as if it lives deep inside our bones. He calls it the desire of the flesh.

Now what does this mean? It's like knowing you should watch your diet, but you still reach for that extra doughnut anyway. It's like knowing you should speak honorably about others, but you still gossip all the same. These are habits, destructive to ourselves and to others, that need to be broken.

But who can help us? This is where the Spirit comes in. Like a personal trainer or a good friend, the Spirit holds us accountable. He helps us break old habits and create new ones that bring peace and produce goodness.

Think about the habits in your life. They may involve certain behaviors or ways of thinking. Think of the good habits; think of the bad. What do you really want to change? Ask the Holy Spirit, in His grace, to train and retrain you. Ask Him to be a good friend, to cheer you on. He will not condemn you, but—if you allow Him—He *will* break the habit.

36

WHY DO YOU WORK?

There is no need, therefore, to blame the body for our sins and vices. This is to slander the Creator. For in its own kind and degree the body is good. But it is not good to abandon the Goodness of the Creator and live for the sake of a created good.

CITY OF GOD, 14.5, TRANS. M. DODS*.

S ome parents have to work really hard to put food on the table. They leave early and come home late. They sacrifice so much in order for their children to have a better life. They miss not being able to see their children more, and sometimes their children do not understand.

As hard as it can be at times, work is still good, even if it takes parents away from their children. Work is good because it provides for those they love.

But what if that same work becomes an end unto itself? What if work is no longer, really, for those they love, but becomes something they love *instead*?

Augustine challenges us to check our priorities. He knows we tend to get things mixed up. We choose something good instead of *the* Good. We love creation but not the Creator. We are too often misaligned, disjointed, and disordered. But God did not intend us to be that way.

Imagine you are having a conversation with Augustine. He asks you about your day, your work, the things you value, and your hopes and dreams for the future. He is not there to judge you. He understands his own struggles all too well. Do your answers reveal a life whose priorities are in the right place? Do they show that you are fully devoted to the people you love? Or has something gone awry?

God loves you because He created you. He doesn't love you because of what you do for Him. In the same way, love God, not for what He made or what He does for you, but for who He is.

37

AN EMOTIONAL
CHECKUP

*The character of the human will, then, is a matter of
concern. If it is out of alignment, the emotions will likewise
be misaligned. But if it is aligned, the emotions will not be
merely blameless, they may even be praiseworthy. For the
will is in them all. Indeed, they are all an expression of the
will. For what are desire and joy but the will's harmony
with the things we long for? And what are fear and sadness
but the will's dissonance with the things we do not want?*

CITY OF GOD, 14.6, TRANS. M. DODS*.

T he *terrific* twos. That's one way of putting it.

Something happens to toddlers around the age of two. Sweet as they have been, and still might be, an earlier moment's peace can quickly descend into an inconsolable storm of emotion. The toddler may be tired or hungry. But mostly, she's starting to figure out there are things she *wants*. She has a *will*. The trouble is communicating that will, and then getting what she wants. Well, actually, that's half the trouble. The other half is being told, "No."

So what do temper tantrums have to do with Augustine? To Augustine, emotions aren't the problem. The problem is the will. Do we make good choices? Do we want ultimately what is right for ourselves?

Augustine says our emotional lives reflect our choices. If our emotions are a mess, then we need to take a good look at the way we order our lives. If our lives are healthy, if harmony abounds, we've likely been making good decisions.

How are you doing, then, emotionally? Let Augustine's words find a place in your heart. Your emotions are not the problem. You don't need to be embarrassed. You don't need to feel ashamed. Just don't ignore them—whatever you do. Ask God to speak through your emotions. Allow Him to work in you, to reinforce what is well-ordered and to rebuild what is broken.

38

ONE LAST CAMPFIRE

And what is pride but the craving for undue exaltation?
Undue exaltation is when the soul abandons the One to
whom it should be joined, the One for whom it is destined,
and becomes a kind of end in itself. This happens when the
soul is satisfied with itself. . . . And this happens when it
falls away from the unchangeable Good that should satisfy
it more than itself . . . and so it grows dim and cold.

CITY OF GOD, 14.13, TRANS. M. DODS*.

A time comes in the autumn for the last campfire of the year. You hope it's not the last, of course. But the days begin to grow shorter and the nights colder. So as the air cools around you, you gather around the fire. It brightens the dark, and it warms hands and faces. The fire brings people together and draws them to the flames.

Perhaps you stoke the fire. Perhaps a marshmallow gets a little too "toasted." The stick in your hand catches alight, a glowing ember at its end. You bring it away from the fire, entertained by the glow and the trails of smoke. The ember doesn't really shed light. It doesn't heat anything. Soon it will only be ash.

For Augustine, God is a bit like that campfire. He brings us together around Himself. He warms us and illuminates the darkness.

Pride, on the other hand, is like the glowing ember taken from the fire. It cannot provide much warmth or light on its own. The ember can barely stay aflame.

Will you say this prayer? *God, help me with my pride. Show me who You are. Show me who I am. Help me find my satisfaction in You, for only in You do I live and move and have my being (Acts 17:28). In Your light, help me shine for those in darkness. In Your heat, help me bring warmth to those in the cold. Amen.*

39

THE DIVINE HEALER

Medical care brings us back to health. God's care heals and restores sinners in a similar way. For just as doctors don't haphazardly bind up wounds, but dress them carefully so that there is a certain beauty as well as utility to the binding, Wisdom likewise adapts its treatment to our wounds by taking up our humanity.

ON CHRISTIAN TEACHING, 1.14.13, TRANS. J. SHAW*.

T hank goodness for modern medicine. When we get sick, we go to the doctor. They identify our illnesses and prescribe what we need to overcome them. When we have severe injuries, we go to the hospital and receive the care we need.

Some wounds cannot be healed by a human doctor. These wounds do not so much afflict the body as harm the soul. They are much more serious. We cannot afford a mistake.

Augustine often talked about sin in these terms. He saw sin as a festering wound, a mortal disease, which needed desperate medical attention. For not only does sin harm us in the short term, but—if left untreated—sin also leads to eternal death.

Only God can properly diagnose and heal sin. He is the Doctor of souls, our divine Healer.

And like a good doctor, God knows exactly what we need. After all, in Jesus, He experienced our suffering firsthand. He knows the causes of our pain; He knows their solutions. His treatments do not produce allergic reactions or cause other troubling symptoms. And when He heals us, He brings beautiful order to the ugly chaos of our spiritual wounds.

Imagine a meeting with the Doctor of your soul. When He asks what He can do for you, describe your spiritual wounds and afflictions. Tell Him your symptoms and your circumstances. Do not hold anything back. You can trust Him. Take His advice, follow His prescriptions, and receive His healing.

40

A DIFFERENT KIND
OF TREATMENT

*A doctor treats a physical wound, in some cases, by applying
contraries—cold to hot, wet to dry, and so on—and in
other cases applies treatments that are similar, such as a
round cloth to a round wound. . . . He does not fit the
same bandage to all limbs, but fits like to like. In a similar
way, the Wisdom of God heals human beings . . . being at
once healer and medicine. Seeing they fell through pride,
He restored them through humility. We were fooled by the
wisdom of the serpent: we are freed by the foolishness of God.*

On Christian Teaching, 1.14.13, trans. J. Shaw*.

econd Kings 5 tells the well-known story of a Syrian general called Naaman. Desperate to be cured of a debilitating skin disease, he sought out the Israelite prophet Elisha, whom he heard had the power to work miracles.

But things did not go as expected. Elisha did not meet him but sent a messenger to tell the general to wash himself seven times in the Jordan River. At first, Naaman angrily refused. He felt it beneath him to do something as simple as bathing in a river. But Naaman's servants changed his mind. Naaman did as Elisha told him, and then he was healed.

Augustine explains that God treats our wounds in different ways. Sometimes things go exactly the way we expect. We have an idea of what we need, and God meets it. Sometimes, however, God does the opposite. His method of healing is a lesson in itself.

Like Naaman, God not only heals our bodies but also heals our pride through humility. He frees us in His "foolishness" from the prisons of our own understanding.

Reflect on the ways God has healed your spirit. Reflect too on areas that still need healing. Ask God to do what is needed, not in the way you want it, or even in the way you might expect. May it be on His terms, not yours. Pray that, in His healing, He will show you more of Himself and how to trust Him more.

THE DOCTOR IS GREATER

He "heals all your diseases." Do not be afraid: every weakness will be restored. They are great, you will say: but the Doctor is greater. The Almighty Physician is able to cure every ailment.

The human physician is sometimes mistaken and promises health in the human body. Why is he mistaken? Because he is not healing what he has created. God made your body, God made your soul. He knows how to restore what He has made.

EXPOSITIONS ON THE PSALMS, 103.4, TRANS. J. E. TWEED*.

D id you ever have an illness that wouldn't go away? No matter what the doctors tried, nothing seemed to work. It can be deeply frustrating. It can also feel like a betrayal of trust. The promise of health didn't come true.

Augustine knows even the best doctors can let you down. They are not all-knowing. They are not all-powerful. And even then, the body they heal once, or even many times, will one day cease to be. We do not live forever.

But God, our divine Healer, will not let us down. Augustine reminds us there is no pain, no suffering in our spirit, He cannot relieve and cure. He made us. He can remake us. He formed us. He can reform us.

Perhaps as you read this devotion, you have become intensely aware of wounds you carry around in your heart, mind, and soul. Some may have been lingering for years. Some you have carried since childhood.

If patterns in your life need to be broken, if some spiritual bones need to be reset, do not resign yourself to the present state of affairs. Do not let fear, especially the fear of disappointment, stop you from seeking healing. It is better by far to be remade by the One who first made you. Trust the Healer.

42

DON'T JUST MAKE DO

You see my strength and my weakness: preserve the one, and heal the other. You see my knowledge and my ignorance. Where You have opened to me, receive me as I enter; where You have closed, open to me as I knock. Let me remember You, understand You, love You.

THE TRINITY, 15.28.51, TRANS. A. W. HADDAN*.

W hen we are seriously sick or hurt, we do not always seek a doctor. Sometimes we see some medical conditions as embarrassing. Other times we treat illnesses and injuries, if manageable, more like inconveniences than reasons to seek medical attention. Maybe we just can't afford to find medical help right now.

So if we can, we put it off. We make do. We believe in our strength to endure, in our wisdom to know how much we can take. After all, painkillers are readily available. Our bodies compensate. So do our minds. But inevitably, whether over a short or long period of time, things begin to break down. Headaches, sleepless nights, and depression—all symptoms arising from unmet needs.

This is as true of the spiritual life as of the physical life. When we are sick in our souls, we show symptoms too. We feel guilt, anxiety, or depression. We know we need help.

Augustine isn't interested in hiding his illness or enduring his injury. God knows anyway. Instead, Augustine lays everything before Him—his strength *and* his weakness; his knowledge *and* his ignorance. He doesn't pretend to have a full bill of health. He knows what he needs. He needs God.

If you have been compensating or just trying to make do, remember God. You don't have to go it alone. But when you call upon Him, don't just give Him your weakness. Give Him your strength as well. Give Him your wisdom as well as your ignorance. Give it all.

43

LIVING TOGETHER

The main purpose for your coming together is to live harmoniously in the house and be of one heart and mind in seeking God. You are not to call anything your own, but have everything in common. Your superior will distribute food and clothing to each of you according to an individual's need, but not equally to all, as all do not enjoy the same health. For as you read in the Acts of the Apostles: "They had everything in common," and "distribution was made to each in proportion to each one's need."

THE RULE OF ST AUGUSTINE, 1.2–3, TRANS. S. WATTS.

T he call to be self-sufficient is everywhere in our society. We can see it on billboards, read it online, and even hear it from friends and family: Independence is good; not needing anything from anyone is good. Yet we wonder why we grow lonelier by the day, finding it ever harder to connect with one another.

We might think Augustine was particularly good at being self-sufficient. After all, he was a "great person," and we usually don't think "great people" need help, let alone a community. But nothing could be further from the truth. Augustine loved to be surrounded by like-minded friends who supported him, challenged him, and kept him honest.

When it came to establishing an intentional Christian community, Augustine sought inspiration from the early church. Everyone was to aim for God-centered unity and harmony. Everything should be shared. But notice everyone isn't treated the same way. This isn't legalism. This is a personal way of life. You need to know the people in your community. You need to know their needs.

God calls Christians to new life. Augustine reminds us this is true not just for individuals, but for communities too. In that spirit, think about those in your community who are presently in need. Ask yourself: *How can I be like Jesus to them today?* But don't stop there. Let someone help you in your need too, whatever it might be. Forget self-sufficiency—give someone the opportunity to be like Jesus to you.

44

DO SOME SPRING CLEANING

The households of those who do not live by faith seek their peace in the earthly advantages of this life. Those households who live by faith, however, look toward the eternal blessings that have been promised. As pilgrims, they use material and temporal things, not to distract or obstruct them from God, but to help relieve the burdens of the corruptible body that weighs upon the soul.

CITY OF GOD, 19.17, TRANS. M. DODS*.

If you've ever moved to a new house, you know the moment well. The moment when you ask yourself the question: *How did I (or we) accumulate all this stuff?*

Sure, some of the stuff is necessary. And some of it you've kept for sentimental reasons. That's fine too. But most of the stuff, which you realize is only taking up space, is really just a symptom of our society. We aren't used to sharing. We also don't *really* like to ask for anything if we can help it. So we equip ourselves with one of everything we could ever need.

Augustine sees that clutter and makes an uncomfortable observation: *You can tell the difference between households of faith and the households of those without faith.*

Why do we have all this stuff? Are possessions an end unto themselves, which we trust will make us secure and happy? Or are possessions a way of easing the burdens of life as we journey toward our eternal goal? The uncomfortable truth is too many of us accumulate possessions as if they are, in fact, the point of living.

It may or may not be spring, but that doesn't mean you can't do some spring cleaning! Cast your mind over what you have in your home, what you have in storage. Why do you have these things? What do they say about what you value? On a journey of faith, do they allow you to travel lightly? Or do they weigh you down? If so, be released.

45

A TRUE MEASURE
OF SUCCESS

*I was planning to live in a monastery with the brothers . . .
having learned what I was planning and hoping to accomplish,
gave me this garden, where the monastery is now. I began
to bring together brothers of good intention, my partners in
poverty. They had nothing, as I did, and were imitating me.*

*I sold my meagre little plot of land and distributed the
money to the poor, and those who wanted to live with me
did the same, so that we could live off of what we shared in
common. And what we held in common was nothing less
than the great and most productive estate of God Himself!*

SERMON 355, TRANS. S. WATTS.

W hat does it mean to be successful? For some it might be loving friendships and a happy family. For others it might be a great career and the adulation of their peers. For others still, it might be a nice house in a good neighborhood, with a healthy retirement package. Perhaps it is some combination of all of these.

It is worth wondering, though, as good as these things certainly are: *Does God have the same measure for success?*

At times throughout the history of faith, including right at the very beginning, a Christian's true success was measured by his or her ability to imitate Jesus even to the point of death. Martyrdom isn't typically what we think of when we think of God's blessing, is it?

In this sermon, Augustine reflects on events that took place many years before. He recalls how his old bishop provided him with the means to start a monastery. With his "partners in poverty," Augustine sought to imitate Christ and His earliest followers the best way they knew how. Augustine even sold his property for the sake of the poor. He chose to live according to a radically different measure of success.

As you spend time in prayer, ask God to reveal His measure of success for your life. It may not be martyrdom. It may not be monasticism. But it might be. And if it is, or something equally radical, do you think you could do it? Do you think you could leave it all behind, like those Galilean fishermen did for Jesus, and follow Him?

46

BE A THOUGHTFUL
GIVER

*Let us say I am given some expensive clothing. It may well
be appropriate for a bishop to wear, but not Augustine—a
poor man from a poor family. People will say I wear
expensive clothes I could not have gotten either when I was
in my father's house or in my earlier secular profession.*

*That's not right. I should only have the kinds of
things I can give to my brother if he is in need.*

SERMON 356, TRANS. S. WATTS.

F ood drives are a wonderful opportunity for a community to provide for those who find it difficult to put food on the table. Understandably, cans of soup or chili are always popular options to give away. They keep. They are easy to cook. But isn't it interesting that what we give at food drives is very different from the food we buy for ourselves?

What we give speaks volumes about what we value. What we give also says a great deal about how much we value the recipients.

In Augustine's time, a bishop had a high social standing. People believed if they got on his good side—i.e., sent a gift his way—he'd provide opportunities for them or their children. Moreover, any self-respecting congregation didn't want their bishop to look embarrassingly shabby.

Augustine, though genuinely thankful, wanted to change the way his congregation thought about giving. An expensive gift was good, but only if it could be sold and given to the poor. Otherwise, the gift implied Augustine was somehow worthier than the other members of his community. Or one might think Augustine only became a pastor because of what he could gain from the position—not because he felt an obligation to serve.

The apostle Paul tells us God loves a cheerful giver (2 Corinthians 9:7). What does your giving say about what and whom you value? What, for instance, does it say about God, who is so generous to you? Be a thoughtful giver as well as a cheerful one.

47

DON'T LET A CHURCH DIVIDE OVER MONEY

The rich, in turn, who were esteemed in the world, must not look down on their brothers who came to this holy community from a life of poverty. . . . They should neither exalt themselves if they contributed something from their resources to the common life, nor take more pride in their riches because they were distributed to the monastery, than if they were being enjoyed in the world.

THE RULE OF ST. AUGUSTINE, 1.7, TRANS. S. WATTS.

The apostle Paul had a problem with the church in Corinth. When they took communion, they were supposed to be united in Christ, no matter who they were or where they came from. But they struggled with leaving their social status and paygrade at the door. The rich got served first; the least in society got crumbs from the table. As far as Paul was concerned, the community may as well pack it in if that was how they were going to behave (1 Corinthians 11:17–22).

It is really difficult for a church, and really any other community, to bring together people from different economic backgrounds. The wealthy and the poor may share the same city, but they live in very different neighborhoods. The same is true of the middle class. And money isn't the only issue. Education, clothes, and cars are other concerns.

Augustine found this tension even within his monastic community. Part of the reason he wanted the brothers to share their goods was so social divisions would not reemerge in the midst of Christian fellowship. Yet those who were rich and gave more to the community than others still thought they were better than those who came from poverty. Pride ruins everything. And old habits are hard to break.

Jesus spoke so often about the dangers of money and the divisions it causes. Spend some time considering how you might help break down this barrier. Ask God to give you a spirit of wisdom and humility. Pray He will help you build bridges across the divide.

48

SO MUCH MORE
BENEATH THE SURFACE

For such is the depth of the Christian Scriptures that, even if I were attempting to study them and nothing else, from early boyhood to decrepit old age, with all the time in the world, the most inexhaustible energy, and abilities greater than I have, I would still be making progress in discovering their treasures.

LETTER 137, TRANS. J. G. CUNNINGHAM*.

id you ever watch one of those nature programs set in the Antarctic? Perhaps the show involved penguins huddling together in subzero temperatures. Were you struck by the sheer beauty of those towering icebergs? Did you pause to wonder how, for all we can see above the surface, so much more is found below?

Augustine views the Bible in a similar way. We may be used to seeing only what is on the page, but he encourages us to look more closely. So much more is beneath the surface. We don't need to be satisfied with just the tip of the iceberg.

The Bible tells us a lot about how to live. But it isn't an instruction manual for a single purpose. The Bible has a particular message for us, of truly good news, but does not always offer a single interpretation. If we believe, as Augustine does, the Bible is the Word of God, then we should prepare to expand our horizons. It is not just a box to check off or a series of questions to answer. The Bible is an unending journey of discovery, where we learn more of God and more of ourselves.

As you pick up your Bible this week, read prayerfully and with expectation. Make greater room in your heart and mind for what God will reveal to you in its pages. Ask God to show you new ways of seeing the familiar. Ask Him to show up in places where you least expect to find Him. May your reading increase your wonder both for the Word and its Author.

49

TRUE TEACHERS

*Let us understand Scripture as Scripture, as God speaking.
Let us not look for human error in its pages. Not for nothing
has the Church established it as canon: this is the work of
the Holy Spirit. If, then, someone reads my book, judge me
carefully: if I have spoken reasonably, do not follow me, but
reason itself; if I have proven something with the most clear
and divine evidence, do not follow me, but Holy Scripture.*

Sermon 162C, trans. S. Watts.

I 'm not sure I've met anyone who wants to relive their teenage years. Many of our parents would agree. One moment, happy preteens enjoy family activities, still under parents' watchful guidance. And the next, they shut themselves in their room or go out with their friends. They respond to parental advice with annoyance if not outright opposition.

Yet finding new role models and authority figures is one of the most important parts about becoming a teenager. That's why if parents want the best for their kids, they hope and pray their kids find good friends, choose good examples to follow, and trust the right people.

Augustine knew a lot of people trusted him. But he was also aware of his many limitations. Like any good teacher, he was still learning. He never wanted those he taught to treat him as some kind of perfect authority figure. He didn't have all the answers, and the answers he gave were not always right.

That is why the Bible was so important to him. Since it was affirmed as the authoritative Word of God (or "canon") by faithful Christians before him, the Bible could be trusted in ways unlike the writings of other men and women.

In a sense, many of us are still like teenagers, eager to find role models we can trust. Remember Augustine's words. A true teacher knows the difference between what they teach and the Truth. They should guide you toward God's Word, not toward themselves and their opinions. Ask God to give you wisdom to discern between those who point toward the Light and those who think they *are* the light.

50

MORE TO DISCOVER

Holy Scripture is composed in a style accessible to all. . . .
A somewhat slow and uneducated mind may not dare
to approach, like a poor man keeping his distance from
the rich; but, by its humble manner, Scripture invites
everyone. It not only feeds all with the plain meaning
of its words but also trains by its hidden truth—having
the same effect in passages both clear and unclear.

Letter 137, trans. S. Watts.

At the beginning of every gold rush, whether it takes place in California, the Yukon, or Ballarat, you find the same sorts of stories. Gold is just lying there on the ground or gleaming on the riverbed. And then word spreads like wildfire. Hundreds, if not thousands of people, arrive from all walks of life. Regardless of who you are or where you're from, the gold's right there for the taking.

But that isn't all there is. For some, the gold on the surface is but a sign of the riches lying beneath the surface. If you are willing to put in the effort, to dig deep down into the earth, rich veins of gold also wait to be discovered. And along the way, precious stones, metals, and minerals too.

For Augustine, the Bible has a similar effect. For many, the Bible is like the beginning of a gold rush. Anyone can open it and discover its treasure. The gold is right there. But for those who wish to follow the golden veins beneath the surface, more is there to discover. Even the Bible's most difficult passages, like an almost unyielding rock, can be mined for precious metals.

Take up your Bible. Pray you will not lose the excitement of discovery. If you are someone who finds gold upon the surface, may the Bible never lose its value in your eyes. If you are someone who desires to dig deeper, may God honor your search with the treasures of His wisdom.

51

"SPEAK, FOR YOUR SERVANT IS LISTENING"

Perfect me, O Lord, and reveal Your secrets to me. Your voice is my joy. Your voice is beyond an abundance of pleasures. Give to me what I love, for I love it.

CONFESSIONS, 11.2.3, TRANS. J. G. PILKINGTON*.

When you think of the voice of God, what comes to mind? The booming voice of some old, bearded man in the heavens? Or something more subtle, something easy to miss if you don't pay close enough attention? Perhaps you think God doesn't actually speak audibly at all. Or if He does, only to very few or to some very special people a long, long time ago.

When Augustine read the Bible, he believed he listened to God's voice. But here's the thing. It was a voice he loved to hear. God's voice gave him great joy. The Bible was not some weighty obligation. Reading the Bible, in a sense, was an opportunity to spend time with a really good friend. The Bible was not a burden. It was a loving gift. Augustine loved spending time reading the Word of God and listening to His voice.

When you read the Bible, do you expect to hear God's voice? Do you believe He truly wants to speak to you, to spend time with you? The truth is, He does. And it's not a one-sided conversation.

The next time you pick up a Bible, before you open the pages, speak the words of a young Samuel in the Old Testament: "Speak, for your servant is listening" (1 Samuel 3:10). And then, listen as you read. What does God say to you? How does He say it? What do you learn about Him as He speaks?

ALL TRUTH IS
GOD'S TRUTH

*Let all good and true Christians understand that wherever
truth may be found, it belongs to their Lord; and while they
recognize and acknowledge the truth, even in pagan religious
literature, let them reject superstitious fictions, and let them
lament and avoid those who, "although they knew God, neither
glorified Him as God nor gave thanks to Him, but their
thinking became futile and their foolish hearts were darkened."*

ON CHRISTIAN TEACHING, 2.18.28 TRANS. J. SHAW*.

F ake news. The phrase seems to be prevalent more and more these days. But the phrase is nothing new. People have always struggled to tell the difference between fact and fiction. Some decide simply to affirm "their truth." Others find the task too difficult and give up trying.

Augustine was not one of these individuals who gave up. He pursued the truth, no matter how difficult. Why? Because he believed finding truth meant finding God.

Augustine wasn't interested in telling "his truth." He was too busy searching for God's truth, wherever it could be found. This meant, for instance, reading Greek and Roman philosophy, literature, and science—the wisdom of his age.

This wasn't as simple as it sounds. The gospel was announced by fishermen, not philosophers. And the Roman society that produced many of these classics was the very same that put Christians to death. What could Christians learn from those who sought their destruction?

Augustine offers a way forward. If all truth is God's truth, then we need not fear the source. We should trust the One who is the source of all truth. He will not lead us astray.

If you worry about the prevailing culture of doubt, be encouraged. You are not the first, and you certainly won't be the last. Ask God to lead you, instead, in determining what can be cast aside, and what can be put to good use. Pray too for the humility to receive wisdom even though it may come from unwelcome places. May wisdom be used for God's purposes, not your own.

53

LEARNING A NEW SKILL

*Wisdom at first ties people up and, by certain laborious
exercises, she trains them. Afterwards, she loosens their bonds,
and gives herself to those she has freed for their enjoyment.
Those she has first trained will thereafter receive her eternal
embraces—and one cannot think of a sweeter or stronger bond.*

LETTER 26, TRANS. S. WATTS.

Often when children learn a new skill—whether it is riding a bike or swimming—some kind of crisis is involved. Either the skill is learned easily, so the child thinks, or will never be learned at all. The adult's responsibility, then, is to offer the necessary encouragement. *You can do this. I know it's difficult now, but with practice, you'll get there.* And it's true. In the end, the child's perseverance pays off.

Augustine offers a similar kind of encouragement. He doesn't, of course, talk about learning to ride a bike. He talks about wisdom, which the book of Proverbs describes as a woman to be sought out, listened to, and obeyed (Proverbs 8). But this wisdom is not won easily. She will make you work for it. You might find it easier to leave her alone, make your excuses, and choose an easier path. But, as Augustine warns, what seems easy at first will only lead to greater hardship further down the road.

We often lose perspective when times get tough. We all want life to be easier at times. If this is where you are, receive Augustine's encouragement. Perhaps others in your life need to hear this encouragement too. The right path is often the most difficult. Don't forget God's perspective. Imagine yourself as that little child learning to ride or swim for the first time. It's not your mom or dad encouraging you on, but your heavenly Father. *It will be worth it in the end.*

54

A LIFE-CHANGING BOOK

*In the ordinary course of study, I came upon a book by
a certain Cicero, whose language, though not his heart,
almost everyone admires. This book of his, Hortensius,
contains an exhortation to philosophy. In fact, this book
changed my affections and turned my prayers to You, O
Lord. It made me have other hopes and desires. Every
vain hope suddenly became worthless to me. And, with an
incredible warmth of heart, I longed for the immortality of
Wisdom, and began to rise so that I might return to You.*

CONFESSIONS, 3.4.7, TRANS. J. G. PILKINGTON*.

D id a book ever change your life? How about an album or a concert? Or perhaps a painting or a film? Many people have these kinds of stories. They start the day looking at the world a certain way, and then they encounter something that shifts their perspective. It can be exciting. It can also be terrifying. Change has a way of doing that!

Augustine experienced some *very* big changes in his life. But this event may have been the one he least expected. He was just going through the motions when he first came across the centuries-old work of Cicero, the famous Roman orator. Augustine was aware of Cicero's impressive reputation. But he also knew he and Cicero shared very different values. What could Cicero say to him about what really mattered? As it turns out, far more than Augustine ever expected. Cicero's book completely transformed Augustine and enflamed his desire for God.

Do you want God to surprise you? Do you want Him to reveal Himself to you in unexpected ways and in unexpected places? Then keep your eyes, ears, and arms open. If you truly seek Him, you will find Him. Don't get so comfortable with your ideas of God that you expect too little of Him and hope He doesn't show you more. Say this prayer: "God, increase my desire for You. Don't let me grow comfortable. Don't let me grow satisfied. Surprise me with more of You."

55

A MIND IS A TERRIBLE THING TO WASTE

Great is this power of memory, exceeding great, O my God—an inner chamber large and boundless! Who has plumbed its depths? . . . A great admiration rises within me; astonishment seizes me. People go out to wonder at the heights of mountains, the huge waves of the sea, the broad flow of the rivers, the extent of the ocean, and the courses of the stars, and fail to wonder at themselves.

CONFESSIONS, 10.8.15, TRANS. J. G. PILKINGTON*.

Sometimes we look in the mirror and don't like what we see. It doesn't help that photoshopped images of unattainable perfection fill our society. So we look down on ourselves and our bodies. Someone is always smarter, funnier, and more successful. Yes, we hear we are special. But even then it's usually just another advertisement trying to sell us something. If we really want to be impressed, we look at someone or something else.

But what if looking isn't the problem? What if we just aren't looking closely enough?

Augustine was the kind of person who paid attention. Occasionally, that gets uncomfortable. Yet with this comes the benefit of seeing things we haven't thought to look for.

Take the human mind, for instance. Augustine asks: *Have you ever considered just how amazing it is? How astonishingly powerful it must be?* It doesn't matter if you did well in school, have a university degree, or feel smart or stupid or somewhere in between. You are the owner of perhaps the most impressive thing in the entire universe. And God, its Creator, gave it to you. So use it well.

Don't take yourself for granted. You are an extraordinary creation, lovingly made. As you look in the mirror, remember who you are, who you *really* are. Instead of looking for what is missing, take a closer look at what's there. May God open your eyes to how He sees you. May He open your heart *and mind* to receive the fullness of His love for you.

56

GOD'S SILENCE PUT INTO SPEECH

When we speak the truth, we use our words to reveal our minds to our listener. We employ these signs to disclose whatever we carry secretly in our hearts so that we can be understood. In a similar way, the Wisdom that God the Father begot is most appropriately named His Word, because the Father's great hiddenness is made known to worthy minds through Him.

On Faith and the Creed, 3.3, trans. S. D. F. Salmond*.

P utting feelings into words can be difficult—especially the feelings that matter most. Our inability to express ourselves can result in heartache. Or just as easily can lead to laughter. Still, we soldier on. At our best, we want to communicate well. And even more than that, we want to know and be made known. We want what is hidden to be revealed and what is hazy to be made clear.

Augustine thought a lot about how we communicate with another, especially how words—even if they just seem a jumble of letters sometimes—speak volumes about who we are. He also thought a lot about how God communicates to us, through Jesus, His Word.

Inspired by the opening passage of the gospel of John, Augustine understood Jesus to be God's fullest self-revelation. God might be utterly mysterious to us, but through Jesus He told us *who He is*. Jesus is therefore not just a particularly good combination of skin and bones. He is God's silence put into speech.

Pick up a Bible and read about Jesus. Perhaps where He talks to the woman at the well (John 4:1–26). Perhaps when He welcomes the tax collector's hospitality (Luke 19:1–10). Or perhaps when He rebukes His disciples for turning children away from Him (Mark 10:13–16). As you read, forget for a moment you are listening to the words of a man called Jesus. You are listening to God Himself.

57

BE VIGILANT

*We need to be on guard with constant vigilance so that we
are not deceived by the appearance of truth, ensnared by
cunning chatter, covered by the shadow of error, made to
believe good is evil or evil is good, hindered by the fear of doing
what we should, or caused by desire to do what we should
not; so that we do not let the sun go down on our anger, let
hatred provoke us to answer evil with evil, let shameful or
immoderate grief consume us, let an ungrateful attitude make
us numb to the blessings we have received, let malicious gossip
worry our good conscience, let rash suspicion deceive us about
another, or let a stranger's false opinion crush our spirit.*

CITY OF GOD, 22.23, TRANS. S. WATTS.

B eing good can be pretty easy sometimes. But it is also a bit like sailing with the wind or swimming with the current. The momentum can lull you into a false sense of security. The wind may become a gust or disappear completely. The current can change direction. If you don't work at your craft or build up your strength, you can get yourself into serious trouble.

Augustine writes to those who consider themselves to be good, faithful Christians. These are the kinds of people who don't think they do anything seriously sinful. But for all they know, they may as well be drifting along with the current. Augustine, ever the pastor, warns his readers to be vigilant.

The beauty of a passage like this draws attention to the kinds of sins a self-righteous person might easily overlook in themselves—self-deception, anger, or an ungrateful heart. These sinful actions, Augustine reminds us, need attention too.

In our prayers, we must ask for more of God's abounding mercy and grace. We all need His help. But this help does not make us passive participants, pulled along by the current, blown about by the wind. His help should fuel our best efforts.

Ask the Lord to give you the endurance to say no to excuses. Pray for vigilance. Pray He will train and prepare you. Pray that you reach your true destination, even if it means swimming upstream.

58

DON'T SIT ON THE SIDELINES

You should not think . . . that you appear in your own eyes to be following God's will, when you are actually unwilling to follow His commandments. One of which, I had only just recalled: "Do not delay to turn to the Lord, do not put it off from day to day." Rather, you should consider things in this way: be confident in His help, and not in your own abilities, to achieve what He has commanded for your eternal salvation. Infirm Firmus, do not hesitate any longer. Commit yourself to Him who is able to do all things. Change your life for the better! Receive the grace of rebirth!

LETTER 2*, TRANS. S. WATTS.

I *'ll get around to it. I promise.* Something needs to be fixed around the house, an appointment needs to be booked, a conversation needs to be started. But for whatever reason, it just doesn't get done. And who doesn't procrastinate from time to time? But just as we aren't always great at getting minor things done, the same can be true of what is most important.

Augustine challenges "infirm" Firmus to get his priorities straight. Firmus says all the right things, but has nothing to show for it. Augustine gets to the heart of the matter. Firmus is unsure. He doesn't trust himself. He doesn't trust God. So he lingers on the sidelines, unwilling to take the literal plunge into the baptized community.

Do you ever find yourself wavering like Firmus regarding spiritual matters? You know the right decision to make, but you are afraid to make it. You put it off, even though you know you shouldn't. How can you overcome this inability to move forward?

Listen to Augustine. *Trust God.* Regardless of the circumstance. If He wants something to happen, it will.

If you don't think you have the strength, lean on Him. He will see you through. God can make a mile out of any single step you take toward Him.

59

SACRIFICE WITH
TRUE INTENTIONS

*There are some who do not drink wine, but instead seek
out liquors fermented from other fruits—not for their
health, mind you, but for their enjoyment. It is as if
Lent was not for the observance of humble devotion, but
rather an opportunity for new kinds of self-indulgence.*

SERMON 210, TRANS. S. WATTS.

T hroughout the long history of Christianity, the season of Lent has played a highly significant role in the church calendar. For forty days, many Christians fast—from meat, alcohol, or something else—in memory of Jesus' suffering and death. Lent is a time of sacrifice and preparation. It is also, in a nutshell, a representation of the Christian experience. Life is difficult. Many temptations are along the way. But if we persevere in faith, we too will be resurrected into new life.

Augustine saw that his congregation knew the routine. No wine though Lent? Check. But he also saw that some had missed the point completely. Instead of drinking wine, they had simply opted for another alcoholic beverage. It was hardly a sacrifice. It was hardly in the spirit of the season.

Augustine was also well aware of the heart's self-deception. He knew how attractive it is to sacrifice one thing, only to attempt to gain something else. But this is not love. It is a transaction. As he wrote time and again, if God is truly our first love, our desires will change. Self-sacrifice will no longer be a show but rather a true expression of our love for the One who sacrificed for us.

Ask God to transform the intentions of your heart. Ask Him to keep your heart in the right place. May your self-sacrifice be an opportunity to love God. May it help you imitate Jesus more fully. May God transform every action from what is "the right thing to do," to what best expresses your love and thankfulness for Him.

DON'T FIGHT FIRE
WITH FIRE

*Why rage against bad people? "Because they're bad," you say.
You add yourself to their number by raging against them.
Let me give you some advice: Are you being bothered by a
bad person? Don't make there be two of you. By condemning
the person, you join them. You increase the number under
judgment. You want to defeat bad with bad and conquer
evil with evil? . . . Have you not heard the Lord's advice:
"Do not be overcome by evil, but overcome evil with good"?*

Sermon 302, trans. S. Watts.

F orest fires are harrowing. They move at high speed, consuming everything in their paths. One minute they are miles away. The next, they are at your doorstep. Sometimes, when conditions are severe enough, two enormous fires can join together in a single conflagration. But rather than burn themselves out, they only grow in ferocity. One can only pray for rain.

We sometimes talk about fighting fire with fire. But most of the time, such as in those great furnaces that burn through bush and forest, this just amounts to a bigger fire.

Augustine talks about anger and condemnation in the same way. Responding to evil with evil only magnifies what was already a terrible situation. It only causes more devastation.

Christians, Augustine makes clear, are not to fight fire with fire. They are not to fight evil with evil. They know another way. As the apostle Paul teaches, only good can conquer evil (Romans 12:17–21). For example, Jesus died for His enemies—He did not kill them. This may be a frustrating message. If there is injustice, we want to lash out. We must, instead, trust the way of our Savior.

Words and actions wound all of us. Think of arguments you've had. How did you respond? Did you fight fire with fire? Did you seek reconciliation? Ask God to redeem it all. Ask Him to prepare your heart for the disagreements to come. May you be one who heals as He heals, not one who wounds. May He grant you His patience and His grace.

61

SEEK GOD FIRST

Listen, you servants and chosen ones of God, you possess the promise of the present and the future. If trials are hard to bear in this life, think about Joseph in prison and Jesus on the cross. If worldly success is close at hand, do not use God for its sake. Use it for God's sake. And do not think His worshippers worship Him because He provides what they need for this life—after all, He gives those things to people who revile Him. Seek first the kingdom of God and His righteousness, and all these things will be given to you.

EXPOSITIONS ON THE PSALMS, 104.40, TRANS. S. WATTS.

One of the most uncomfortable facts about Christianity is this: not only did Jesus suffer a gruesome death, but only one of His closest followers appears to have died of natural causes.

Following God can sometimes lead to great hardship. Jesus even told His followers to expect trouble (John 16:33). If only He had promised things would get easier. If only He had said you will fulfill all your dreams in this life and gain access to heaven in the process.

Augustine knew life could be very difficult—almost unbearable—for many people. He also knew some people seem to prosper without a care in the world. That's life. Bad things happen to good people. Good things happen to bad people. As Augustine reminds us, however, those whom God chooses can look to the future in hopeful expectation, whatever their lot in life. Just remember, God isn't something we use to get to our destination. We don't use God for our purposes; He uses us for His purposes.

May God give you an eternal perspective each passing day. Whether in health or sickness, happiness or grief, prosperity or lack, may you truly seek Him first. If you feel at times God has not met your needs, remember He chose you for so much more than what the world offers. Seek God. Trust in Him. He will provide.

62

FOR THOSE
RESTLESS NIGHTS

Set me free, O God, from the multitude of words that inflict me in the depths of my soul, which is wretched in Your sight and takes refuge in Your mercy. For I am not silent in my thoughts, even when I am silent in my words.

THE TRINITY, 15.28.51, TRANS. A. W. HADDAN*.

D o you ever have those nights where you just can't get to sleep? Your head hits the pillow and then, at the very moment your eyes close, the worries of the day *and* the worries of tomorrow come crowding into your head like many noisy, unwanted guests.

Mental health sounds like an especially modern concern. It isn't. Like Augustine, many throughout the ages recognized our minds often seem like battlefields. They knew a person may appear to be at peace while a battle rages within.

Consumed by destructive thoughts and constant worries, our minds race and we struggle to keep up. And what is worse, our attempts to control our minds only seem to make us more anxious.

Augustine knew he needed help. He wanted an end to the great "multitude of words" that afflicted his soul. He sought silence for that endless crowd of busy thoughts. If only he could be still. If only he could be at peace. He needed God's mercy. He needed God's silence.

Sometimes all we want is for God to speak. We want Him to speak so loudly that He drowns out all the other voices that rattle around in our heads. But perhaps what we really need is God's silence: a peace that calms the raging seas, a hushed stillness that falls upon a crowded room.

Is this what you need? Is this what you listen for? If so, say this prayer: "Lord, have mercy. I cannot do this without You. Be my peace. Be my rest. Be my refuge. Amen."

KEEP YOUR ENGINE
RUNNING SMOOTHLY

The Doctor gave us orders when we were healthy . . . so that we would not need Him. "It is not the healthy who need a doctor, but the sick." When we were healthy, we chose to ignore His orders. We have since learned from experience what a disaster that turned out to be. Now we are getting sick, oppressed, and are laid out on our sick bed—but we should not lose hope.

Since we are unable to go to the Doctor, He has decided to come to us. Although He was ignored by the healthy, He does not ignore the afflicted.

SERMON 88, TRANS. S. WATTS.

S ome people buy cars they plan to run into the ground. They are usually vehicles they didn't spend much money on. As long as the cars get from A to B and don't require much upkeep, the owners are content. Of course, things rarely go as planned. Cars need checkups and oil changes. They need new brakes and tires. As expensive and as time-consuming as these kinds of things are, listen to your mechanic and get the work done. Otherwise, sooner or later, you'll find yourself on the side of the road, smoke billowing from the engine.

Augustine, of course, knew nothing about cars. But he knew a lot about people. And he knew most people, as long as they feel healthy, don't think to visit a doctor. Sometimes they don't even follow their doctor's advice if it's too inconvenient.

The same goes for the spiritual life. If we feel spiritually healthy, or at least *healthy enough*, we feel we don't need to spend time with God. But then something happens. Our lives take a turn for the worse. We break down. And there we are, stuck, like a broken-down car on the side of the road. Thank God He doesn't wait for our arrival. He comes to us.

Do you feel healthy? Do you feel as if you are just hanging on, hoping and praying you'll reach your destination? Do you listen to the Doctor's advice? Pray God will speak, and you will listen. Ask Him to help you put in the work now, whatever the cost. Don't wait any longer.

64

A BAD HAIR DAY

Pride is the source of all afflictions, because pride is the source of all sins. If when removing a disease from the body a physician merely cures the symptoms and not the cause itself, the patient will only seem to be healed for a time. But while the cause remains, the disease will reappear.

Cure pride and there will be no more evil. This is why the Son of God came down from heaven and was made humble.

Tractates on the Gospel of John, 25.16, trans. J. Gibb*.

A bad hair day isn't going to get fixed by a different shirt or dress. You can put sunglasses on if you like. Maybe even a hat. It isn't really going to change a thing.

This may seem a silly analogy at first, but isn't this how so many of us deal with our problems? Instead of looking directly into the mirror and admitting the truth, we go about trying to fix everything else. We may even get angry if others point out our issue. But we want them to ignore it—just like we try to do.

Pride is the source of all afflictions. Pride assumes the world should revolve around us. Pride acts as if other people's well-being is always secondary to our own. Pride believes God is inessential to our happiness. Instead of getting to the root of the problem, we do the equivalent of changing our shirt or wearing sunglasses. We put on a good front, yet still wonder why the world remains full of anger and sorrow.

May God help us take off the bandages we have been putting over our spiritual wounds.

If you are ready for a change, are tired of appearances, and want to get to the heart of the matter, will you pray? "God, please heal me. Heal my pride with Your humility. Help me to let go. Do what You need to do to make me whole again. Although I may be afraid, You know what You are doing. Amen."

OUT OF TUNE

*Humanity's nature was created faultless and without
sin. This nature, however, in which everyone is born of
Adam, now requires a doctor, because it is unhealthy. All
the good qualities it still possesses in its form, life, senses,
and intellect, is due to its Creator and Maker, the Most
High God. But the flaw, which darkens and weakens
all those natural goods so that it needs illumination
and healing, has not been contracted from its faultless
Creator—it is from original sin, committed by free will.*

ON NATURE AND GRACE, 3, TRANS. P. HOLMES AND R. E. WALLIS*.

If you ever play music or listen to it carefully, you know if an instrument doesn't sound quite right. A string may be a little sharp or flat. Sometimes, however, the problem is more serious. The instrument is severely damaged and won't stay in tune, causing it to be unlistenable.

When Augustine writes about what happened to humanity, it's as if he is referring to an instrument that has lost its ability to stay in tune. When the instrument was first carefully and lovingly crafted, it played in beautiful harmony with itself and every other instrument. But then something happened. After that, even at its best, the instrument didn't sound as rich as its design would suggest.

So what happened? Humanity freely chose a different way from the one intended by its Creator. And ever since, much like a damaged instrument, it never quite stayed in tune. Sometimes it sounds pretty good—other times it sounds terrible. But humanity cannot reach the harmony for which it longs.

As Augustine reminds us, this was not the fault of the One who made us. It was a decision we made and continue to make for ourselves.

Would you offer this prayer? "God, our Father and Maker, we need You to undo what we have done. You have made us to resonate with Your divine music. We were meant to be in harmony with You and Your creation. But we have fallen out of tune. Forgive us. And, in Your mercy, repair us. Make us new."

66

THE KINGDOM OF HEAVEN IS NOT A DEMOCRACY

"Is God unjust? Not at all!" Why, then, do things happen in this way and not in another? "O human, who are you?" If you do not have to repay your debt, be grateful. If you have to repay it, you have no reason to complain. We must only believe, even if we are unable to understand it, because He who made and fashioned every creature, spirit, and body, arranges all things according to their number, weight, and measure.

TO LETTER TO SIMPLICIANUS, TRANS. S. WATTS.

I n a democracy, government officials should be accountable to the people they represent. They are elected, which means they can also be voted out of office. The people have the final authority—or at least they are supposed to.

God, however, is not an elected official. The kingdom of heaven is not a democracy.

God isn't a tyrant either. The Bible is full of examples where the faithful plead their cases before Him, ask questions about what He is doing, and seek to understand the wisdom of His decisions. Sometimes He provides answers—even if they are a long time coming. Sometimes we just need to trust Him. In the end, we are not the final authority.

When it comes to seeking answers, and especially about those issues that seem most unjust and unfair, Augustine wants us to start from the right place. We must begin by affirming that God is just, God is wise, and He is our Creator. Whatever happens, these facts remain true. So even when a great injustice takes place, it does not follow that God is now unjust. We simply don't see the whole picture. And as frustrating as it might be, He is under no obligation to show us.

Whatever may happen, do not forget where you stand. Start with what you know to be true of God. But that doesn't mean you shouldn't ask questions. *Do* ask questions. Make your complaints. Just pray you don't lose your bearings. Even if you don't understand what's going on, He does. And for that, and so much more, He deserves your praise, come what may.

67

ENJOY THE ORDINARY
THINGS IN LIFE

*People, busy with other things, no longer consider the works
of God, for which they should daily praise Him as Creator.
For this reason God has reserved to Himself, as it were,
certain extraordinary actions, so that by these amazing
events He might awaken them, as from a sleep, to worship
Him. A dead man rises; people marvel. So many are born
each day, and no one marvels. If we reflect more carefully,
it is a matter of greater wonder for one to be who was not
before, than for one who was to come to life again.*

TRACTATES ON THE GOSPEL OF JOHN, 8.1, TRANS. J. GIBB*.

F amiliarity breeds contempt. The same streets, the same people—we may love and appreciate them, but we can get so *used to them*. We take them for granted. The magic is gone.

This problem is compounded in the digital age. Society trains us to value what is new and exciting. Everything grows brighter and louder to gain our attention. Our attention spans shorten as a result. We want the next thing, and the next thing after that.

Who knows what Augustine would have thought of our digital culture? He would probably tell us to get off our phones and take a good look around.

The world is a miraculous place. Every detail, every inch of life, should inspire wonder at the work of the Creator's hands. Sure, some events seem more extraordinary than others. Yet Augustine reminds us that something as common as childbirth is a truly miraculous event that should inspire awe in God.

If you find the world has become too familiar and you have lost your sense of wonder, say the following prayer or use it as a springboard to create your own: "Lord, give me new eyes to see. Show me just how extraordinary the ordinary *really* is. Help me be grateful for each moment, and for each day. Amen."

68

GOD ISN'T A MAGICIAN

One should not be amazed God worked a miracle. A miracle is amazing only if it is performed by a human being. We should rejoice, then, that our Lord and Savior Jesus Christ was made human, rather than be amazed at the miracles He performed among human beings. It is of greater importance to our salvation that He was made for humans, than what He did among them. It is more significant that He healed the vices of souls, than that He healed the ailments of bodies destined to die.

TRACTATES ON THE GOSPEL OF JOHN, 17.1, TRANS. J. GIBB*.

God performs amazing feats. That is just what He does. But to quote a well-known literary character, do not take Him for a conjurer of cheap tricks.

Of course, we don't think of God as someone who pulls rabbits from a hat. But we might be tempted, from time to time, to expect Him to put on a show. In fact, the devil tried to convince Jesus to do that very thing. He refused (Matthew 4:1–11).

God isn't interested in manipulating us. He isn't interested in impressing us. He is not here for our entertainment.

Augustine tells us the right response to God is not amazement, even though He truly is amazing. The right response is joy—the kind of joy that emerges from a deep sense of gratitude. For God didn't come to us in Jesus to put on a show; He came to save us. The miracles He performed on people's broken bodies, as impressive as they were, pale in comparison to the healing He works in our souls every day. For Augustine, the equation is simple. One is eternal; the other is passing away.

May God bless you with a deeper appreciation for Jesus. May He bless you with a greater understanding of the work He does in your life. Pray your desire to be amazed will be transformed into a desire to be thankful. Seek joy rather than entertainment. *Lord, show me what really matters.*

HE IS MORE BEAUTIFUL

The world is loved: but He should be preferred over the world He has made. The world is great: but He is greater than the world He has made. The world is beautiful: but He is more beautiful than the world He has made.

SERMON 96, TRANS. S. WATTS.

The world is full of astonishing beauty. From its winding rivers and wooded valleys to its great deserts and towering peaks, its natural splendor can take the breath away. And what of its creatures? Numerous species of every size and color fill us with delight. And last but not least, we should not forget about human beings. So many varied cultures span the globe, each full of creativity and artistry.

"God so loved the world that he gave his one and only Son . . ." (John 3:16).

Augustine loved the world too. He knew and deeply appreciated its greatness and its beauty. When he began his monastic community, he wasn't motivated by a fear of the world. He just knew he should never love the world at the expense of the Creator.

Augustine also knew that however great the world is, God is greater. He is more beautiful, more worthy of our love. Creation, then, is not a temptation. It gives us a foretaste of who God really is. Whatever we experience in this world that is good, true, and beautiful: He is better, truer, and more beautiful.

Bring to mind all you love and appreciate in the world around you. What are you thankful for? What inspires you? What fills you with wonder? May these thoughts lead you to contemplate Him—He who is greater than a mountain, more radiant than the sun.

70

A JUST WAR

*How many great wars, how much human carnage
and bloodshed, have been necessary for this peace?
And while these conflicts took place in the past, we
have not yet seen the end of such miseries.*

*If I attempted to give an adequate description of warfare's
many, varied, and evil disasters, these hard and dreadful
difficulties . . . I could begin, but where would I end?
They say a wise ruler will only wage just wars. But
if a ruler remembers their humanity, surely they will
deplore the necessity of waging even just wars.*

CITY OF GOD, 19.7, TRANS. S. WATTS.

War is a truly horrible thing. It kills and maims. It destroys and displaces.

War is a terrible price to pay for peace. But sometimes that is what peace costs. The aggressor must be defeated. But almost anything is better than more conflict.

Augustine is well-known for his reflections on what is now called the "Just War" theory. He tried to understand, as a follower of Jesus, what needed to happen for a war to be *just*. As we read here, however, he clearly wished a reason to go to war never existed in the first place. But if war needs to happen, it must be for legitimate reasons. Violence must be limited at all costs. A just war must never aim to dominate, but, rather, to reconcile.

Jesus said: "Love your enemies and pray for those who persecute you" (Matthew 5:44). Was He wrong? Did He not understand the complexities of politics and the human heart? Hardly. Let us, then, be peacemakers first and foremost. May we never forget God lovingly created even our bitterest opponents. And even in the event we are drawn into conflict, let us do so only for the sake of peace and for the sake of seeing those who were once our enemies become our friends.

FALSE ADVERTISING

And so I fell among men who were delirious with pride, much too sensual and talkative. The devil's snares were in their mouths, a sticky concoction mixed with the syllables of Your name, the name of our Lord Jesus Christ, and the name of the Paraclete, our Comforter, the Holy Spirit. These names did not leave their mouths, but as far as the sound and racket of their speech was concerned, their hearts were empty of truth.

CONFESSIONS, 3.6.10, TRANS. S. WATTS.

W ho hasn't fallen for false advertising at one time or another? The seller says all the right things. Everything we want to hear. The deal is good, almost too good to be true. And then, sure enough, we find out it is. We feel frustrated, even angry. No one likes to be taken advantage of. Nobody wants to find out what he or she believes to be true is actually a lie.

Augustine had the same experience among a group called the Manicheans. As a young man, he was attracted to a lot of what they had to say. The Manicheans seemed to have an understanding of what was *really* going on in the world. And, even better, they said all the right things. They spoke about Jesus and the Holy Spirit.

When Augustine finally got to talk to one of their leaders, however, he realized the wool had been pulled over his eyes. He thought he had gained access to the truth, a truth only a few of the most enlightened could see. But he had been swindled.

The world is full of false advertising—particularly in spiritual matters. But how can we learn from Augustine? How can we discern between what is true and what is false?

Pray God will give you wisdom. Ask Him to give you ears to hear and eyes to see. Learn to ask good questions. Listen carefully. And, most importantly, measure what you hear against what you see. Do the words match the behavior? Are they spoken in pride or in humility? Do they point to what Jesus said about Himself?

LOVE ONE ANOTHER

Every day we are greeted with bowed heads because we resolve disputes over gold, silver, land, and flocks. Yet it is over our Head Himself that this utterly shameful and destructive conflict exists between us. However low those who greet us bow their heads, so that we might reconcile them in earthly matters, our Head lowered Himself from heaven even to the cross. Yet we are not reconciled in Him.

LETTER 33, TRANS. S. WATTS.

A new command I give you: Love one another. As I have loved you, so you must love one another. By this everyone will know you are my disciples, if you love one another" (John 13:34–35).

Augustine lived in a city divided between two hostile Christian communities. Both saw themselves representing the true faith. The cause of the division went back generations. The local government had persecuted the church, even killing some of its leaders. In dealing with the trauma, two different sides emerged, holding distinct opinions on how to move forward. But in committing to their opposing sides and justifying the division that appeared within the church, they flatly ignored Jesus' fundamental commandment: "Love one another." As Augustine points out, the church leaders who were supposed to be reconciling people to God were not even reconciled to one another or to Jesus—the head of the Church.

Does this sound familiar to you? You do not need to have lived in ancient North Africa to recognize this kind of behavior. But note how the division arose from a deeply painful experience. Deep healing is needed. It is going to take work. It is going to be ugly. Do you want to be someone who follows Jesus' commandment even when the situation is messy? Are you willing to work for reconciliation? Is there someone you need to call?

73

LOVE IN ACTION

You do not have love, because you divine unity for the sake of your own reputation. Now, this is how you learn to discern whether or not a spirit is from God. Pick up clay pots and tap them, perhaps they rattle and sound badly. See if they resound clearly, see if love is there. You remove yourself from the unity of the whole earth, you divide the Church by schisms, you tear the Body of Christ into pieces. He came in the flesh to gather; you cry out to scatter. This, therefore, is the Spirit of God, the One who says Jesus has come in the flesh: Not in speech, but in actions; not by making sounds, but by loving.

HOMILIES ON THE FIRST EPISTLE OF JOHN, 6.13, TRANS. S. WATTS.

T alk is cheap. Calling for dialogue is one thing, but listening to what another person has to say is much harder. Collaboration, unity, friendship, and community are all just empty words if there's no real intention of putting them into practice. How can we say we are full of love for all people if we never even consider inviting people into our homes to share a meal?

Augustine was fed up. He'd had enough of empty words. Jesus had sacrificed too much to be represented by those who were effectively trying to undo everything He had accomplished. Jesus brought people together, but His so-called followers were pulling them apart. Didn't they know it was His body they were tearing to pieces?

Augustine reminds us God did not just tell us what to do. Jesus showed us. He is God's Word put into action. And if the Holy Spirit dwells within us, we will also show love in our actions.

Think of someone to invite to your house this week or the next. Someone who isn't already one of your close friends but could probably do with some hospitality. And what about that other person, the one you had a falling out with? What would it look like to imitate Jesus in that relationship?

Will you say this prayer? "God, make us whole. Take our words and make them real by the power of Your Spirit. Amen."

74

NO ONE GETS IT
ALL RIGHT

*For I have now begun to go back over my writings, in order
to show that even I have not followed myself in all things.
But I think, with God's mercy, I have made progress in
my writing. I did not begin from a state of perfection.
Indeed, I would speak more arrogantly than truly if I said
even now, at my present age, I had arrived at perfection,
without any error in what I write. There is a difference,
however, in the nature and subject of an error and how
easily it is corrected, or how stubbornly it is defended.*

On the Gift of Perseverance, 21.55, trans.
P. Holmes and R. E. Wallis*.

As we grow older we become less open to having our minds changed. We get tired of disagreement. Or maybe we don't want to change our ways, even if we know we don't have everything right. Change requires too much effort.

Toward the end of his life, Augustine went back over the mountain of books he had written over the previous decades. As he read, he found he had gotten some teachings wrong or made other teachings unclear. Even as he continued to hold strong opinions about what he thought was true, he never confused himself with the Truth. There was always room for improvement.

Augustine shows us we are all works in progress. Only the proud think they have nothing else to learn.

Let us not be defensive, whether it is about something we think we know or about something we know next to nothing about. Let us choose, instead, to be humble. Rather than confusing a lie for the truth, being humble will help us remain ever open to receiving God's wisdom.

Give yourself the opportunity to learn something new. Even better, look into something you ordinarily wouldn't be interested in. Get out of your comfort zone. Be vulnerable. If it is God's job, and not yours, to be all-knowing, what have you got to lose?

75

START THE
CONVERSATION

The person who confesses to You does not teach You what goes on within them. A closed heart is not closed to Your eye. A hard heart does not repulse Your hand. Instead, you soften it when You want to, either in pity or in vengeance.

CONFESSIONS, 5.1.1, TRANS. J. G. PILKINGTON*.

*N*o *I didn't.* The child was defiant. His parent looked over at his younger sister sobbing on the floor. *You did. I saw what happened.*

Even when pretending is useless, it can be hard to admit the truth when we are caught. Maybe we think we can still get away with it. Maybe we have a hard time admitting to ourselves what we did. The lie only makes it worse.

Augustine knew we can't hide anything from God. When He looks at us, He sees everything. Even the things we'd much rather He didn't see. We might think this is all too much. We want our privacy. Who wants to be held accountable for *every single thing*?

This would be understandable if God's desire was to control us or to cover us with shame. But that's not His desire. Whether in showing compassion or punishment, He is our loving Father.

When we finally decide to tell the truth and confess to Him our sin, we may find ourselves surprised. We don't tell Him anything He doesn't already know. Instead, we start the conversation. And, over its course, we learn more about Him and about ourselves. His love gradually replaces our fear and anger.

Are you holding anything back from God? Something you don't want to tell Him? Here's the good news. *He already knows.* He isn't interested in catching you and kicking you when you're down. He doesn't hold grudges. Hear and see the truth. Receive forgiveness. Be released.

GOD'S STANDARD
OF BEAUTY

Let us return, then, and listen to what He said. And,
as I said, let us examine ourselves. Whatever we find
missing, let us cultivate with great care, according to
the standard of beauty that is pleasing in His sight.
And, because we are not able to do it by ourselves, let
us ask Him for help. May the God who formed us, re-
form us. May the God who created us, re-create us.

SERMON *301A*, TRANS. S. WATTS.

Oh, the hectic nature of family portraits. *You, stand over there. You, sit still. Okay, look over here. Wait, have you brushed your hair?* Just getting the children to sit still and look in the same direction at the same time is a minor miracle. But then the universe aligns, and the photographer takes the picture. The portrait is beautiful. Congratulations, you immortalized a fleeting moment of utter perfection.

Getting everything to meet our own expectations of what is well-ordered and beautiful is hard. That is why we take the picture. Well-ordered beauty is pretty much impossible to sustain in real life.

Augustine isn't especially interested in keeping up appearances, however. When he talks about God's standard of beauty, he isn't referring to how we look. He talks instead about what really matters, about how we live day to day. He knows taking a hard look at ourselves is difficult enough, let alone doing anything about it. That is why we need God. Not only is His standard of beauty the only one that counts, but He is also the only One who helps us attain it. And the way He looks at us will stand the test of time.

Read the Gospels and take the words of Jesus to heart. These are God's standard of beauty. These are His account of a well-ordered life. If you find them too difficult, pray He will help your efforts. Ask Him to reform you, even to re-create you. Pray the change He makes in you will be everlasting.

77

GOD ISN'T SANTA CLAUS

God's patience still invites the wicked to repent, even as His scourge trains the good in patience. Similarly, God's mercy embraces the good in order to nurture them, as His severity restrains the wicked to punish them. Divine Providence has chosen to prepare good things for the righteous in the world to come, which the unrighteous will not enjoy. And as for the wicked, they will receive pains that will not afflict the good.

CITY OF GOD, 1.8, TRANS. M. DODS*.

S anta Claus has a list. Or so the story goes. And on that list are the names of all the children of the world, the naughty and the nice. One group gets coal; the other gets presents. But has anyone actually met a child who received a piece of coal? Of course not. Santa Claus wouldn't be so mean.

We all know Santa Claus isn't real, and every Christmas season, we should remember the real meaning of Christmas. Jesus was born so that through His death and resurrection we would be set free from the eternal consequences of our sin. But even as we hear that message time and again, don't we still have a tendency to imagine God as a bit more like Santa? Sure, there are naughty and nice kids. But everyone gets a present in the end.

Augustine's account of God is much more uncomfortable. And also much more faithful to the Bible. And really, if we are honest, Augustine's account is more consistent with our experience of the world. All too often, the nice suffer while the naughty get the presents. Even the Christmas season itself can be very difficult for many. Hope and good cheer are not so easily bought.

Let the Bible tell you who God is, even if it makes you uncomfortable.

Say this prayer: "Lord, thank You for patiently allowing the wicked to repent. Lord, thank You for using suffering to build the endurance of the faithful. Lord, help us not to lose sight of eternity even as we struggle to see things clearly in the present."

78

HERE TODAY AND GONE TOMORROW

"The life of mortals is like grass." Let a person consider who they are; let no one be proud. Their days are like grass. Why should grass be proud? It flourishes now but will soon wither. It is in flower only for a brief time until the sun grows hot. It is good, then, that God's mercy is upon us. From grass, He makes gold.

EXPOSITIONS ON THE PSALMS, 103.19, TRANS. J. E. TWEED*.

M ost young people seem to think they'll live forever. Death, for the most part, isn't on their radar. *That, they think, is what happens to the old.* This partly explains their choice in tattoos. The thought doesn't occur to them that whatever looks good in their twenties may not look quite the same in forty or fifty years. But even the old, unless they have a close brush with death, can think this way too. Coming to terms with the end is difficult.

Augustine isn't trying to make people feel insignificant or disposable. He is, however, telling us to get real. In the grand scheme of things, we are here and we are gone.

But there is hope. We are not chained to the cycles of birth and death. For even if our lives are much like grass, God's mercy rests upon us. He will take that perishable straw and make imperishable gold.

Do you fear getting old? Do you fear getting sick? Do you want to *mean* something when all is said and done?

Here is the truth: The end will come. But you don't need to be afraid. Let go of your pride. Stop trying to control the uncontrollable. You are never self-sufficient.

Receive God's mercy instead. Feel it rest upon you. Enjoy its comfort. Your life may be like a blade of grass that is here today and gone tomorrow, but in your Creator's hands it will be made golden.

79

BUILD YOUR HOUSE
ON THE ROCK

*Although good and bad people suffer alike, we must
not think there is no difference between them because
the cause of their suffering is the same. For even in the
similarity of their sufferings, there remains a dissimilarity
in the sufferers. . . . For as the same fire causes gold
to glow brightly, and straw to smoke . . . so the same
violence of suffering proves, purges, and purifies the
good, but damns, devastates, and destroys the wicked.*

CITY OF GOD, 1.9, TRANS. M. DODS*.

Why me? Very few of us think we deserve to suffer. We might have an injury or illness. Perhaps a friend betrayed us or a relationship broke down. But here's the thing: suffering happens to everyone. We all suffer, regardless of our circumstances. Regardless of how good or bad we've been. Regardless of whether we think we deserve it.

Augustine takes suffering as a given. The key is what happens when we suffer. How do we respond? What does it reveal about who we really are? When suffering comes in waves, the virtuous are left battered, but they remain standing. As the parable goes, they built their house on the rock. Those who built on a less sure foundation are swept away (Matthew 7:24–27).

This is all much easier said than done. Believing this truth is one thing—clinging to this belief in times of great difficulty is much harder. If you are suffering at the moment, I encourage you not to think about whether or not you deserve it. Reflect instead on how God might be using this season to purify you and to strengthen your dependence on Him.

But what if things are otherwise going well? Prepare yourself for the inevitable. Trouble is coming. And when those waves wash over you, will you trust in God's strength or your own? Is your foundation secure?

80

DISCOVERING GOD'S INTENTIONS

*We have no doubt that to increase and multiply
and replenish the earth, in accordance with
God's blessing, is a gift of marriage, which God
instituted from the beginning before the Fall.*

*It is quite clear they were created male and female, with
bodies of different sexes, for the very purpose of increasing,
multiplying, and replenishing the earth by becoming
parents. It would be utterly absurd to deny so plain a fact.*

CITY OF GOD, 14.22, TRANS. M. DODS*.

T he concept may seem strange to us now, but when Augustine lived, the ideal Christian wasn't the kind of person who got married, stayed married, and had a few children along the way. Rather, the ideal Christian was someone who refused marriage and stayed celibate. Some believed such people were the closest thing to angels. They were models of holiness who radically broke from the sexualized culture of the age. In fact, their particular sexuality had no meaningful bearing on their identity. How things have changed!

Augustine, however, had no fears about pointing out the obvious. He believed men and women were, biologically speaking, substantially different. And this difference ultimately amounted to their ability to produce children together. This was no biological accident or something to be set aside for some other desire. This, Augustine firmly believed, was clear evidence of God's intention. If the Creator made men and women this way, who are we to disagree?

Life can get complicated. In fact, the more you try to figure out things for yourself, the more complicated and confusing life will get. After all, you are not your own maker. If you crave some much-needed clarity about God's intentions about a matter, now may be time to find some help. Pray God will speak to you clearly, that His words will be like a ray of light cutting through a dense fog. Ask Him to bring wise and experienced people into your life to guide you. May God give you eyes to see His intentions and a heart to accept them in humility.

81

THE HEAVENLY CITY

The heavenly city, while it sojourns on earth, invites
citizens from every nation and gathers them together
into a pilgrim society of all languages. It is not worried
about the diversity in customs, laws, and institutions
that secure and maintain human peace. . . . Rather than
rescinding or abolishing these differences, it actually
preserves and adopts them, provided only they do not
hinder the worship of the one supreme and true God.

CITY OF GOD, 19.17, TRANS. M. DODS*.

T here is neither Jew nor Gentile, neither slave nor free, nor is there male and female, for you are all one in Christ Jesus" (Galatians 3:28).

The apostle Paul wrote these words to a community of Christians trying to figure out how a predominantly Jewish faith could incorporate people who are Gentiles—i.e., people who aren't Jews. If you have faith in Jesus Christ, Paul explained, you become one of God's children. It doesn't matter who you are or where you come from. No one gets special treatment.

Augustine develops the point further. The heavenly city, which comprises followers of Christ, invites everyone in. But here's the thing: When you become a follower of Christ, you also become a pilgrim. You become homeless, just as Jesus was homeless. What defines you in the earthly city no longer defines you in the heavenly. Yet that does not mean your ethnic identity is worthless. Instead, insofar as your ethnicity seeks human peace and does not challenge the true faith, it should be embraced, no matter its origin.

Do you feel like a pilgrim? And if other pilgrims join you on your way, are you equally welcoming, regardless of their ethnicity, class, or gender? You are all on your way to the same heavenly city. Be unified on your journey.

82

BE GRACIOUS TO OTHERS

The Church is great. Everyone loves each other.
Everyone does all they can for one another.

People come, drawn by these praises, only to find bad
people within the congregation who were not mentioned
before they arrived. And so they take offense at false
Christians, and run away from those who are true.

And then there are the hateful and slanderous who rush
to blame Christians. . . . "Who are Christians? They
love money. . . . They are drunks, gluttons, envious,
and backbiters." This is true of some, but not of all.

EXPOSITIONS ON THE PSALMS, 100.9, TRANS. J. E. TWEED*.

T rue fans know. They live and die with their teams. A brief winning streak and they are all but assured of a championship. A few losses and everyone needs to get traded or fired. Keeping a steady course is hard, especially when you are passionate about something. People seem more attracted to strong opinions anyway.

Augustine never expected Christians to be perfect. He knew himself too well. But he also didn't entertain the other extreme. Mostly because it wasn't true. If anything, Christians are really bad at PR. On one hand, we try to make ourselves look better than we are. On the other, we aren't nearly as bad as others say.

As Augustine observed, the Church is a mix of the good and the bad, much like the rest of the world. We might find this incredibly frustrating. But be thankful for the grace of God. He is patient with us, even if we are impatient with each other. In fact, tolerating other Christians who frustrate us is part of what it means *to be* a Christian.

Consider your Christian community. What is the relationship between who they say they are and who they *really* are? Think, too, about yourself. Is a similar dynamic at work? Are you as gracious to those in your community as you are to yourself? God is more gracious still. So then, be encouraged. Don't pay attention to those loud voices, at least no more than is necessary. Seek instead to be as gracious to others as God is to you.

FAITH IN ACTION

I beg you, for the sake of your Christian charity, that
these things I have written to your love are not in vain.
The Galatians have powerful friends. With their support
they demand we return those the Lord liberated by means
of the church—even those who have returned to the
friends and families who had been looking for them.

LETTER 10*, TRANS. S. WATTS.

The ancient world took slavery for granted. Some people, due to economic distresses, became slaves or sold their children into slavery—at least for a period of time. Enslaving free-born citizens against their will, however, was forbidden. But as is typically the case when a profit is to be made, some tried to get away with it anyway. Much like human traffickers today, ancient slavers abducted men, women, and children. They then passed them along to others, who would sell the slaves in distant provinces—far away from home.

Augustine's church found out 120 trafficked people were being held in the city harbor. Some of its members decided to break them out. It was not unusual for Christian congregations to buy the freedom of the enslaved, but this was a radical step. The church then housed and fed as many of the freed slaves as they could. But the slavers came knocking. They wanted their *merchandise* back. They even got some of their powerful friends involved. That's why Augustine wrote to an influential friend of his own. The church needed all the help it could get.

This is a stirring account of Christian charity. It puts faith into action *courageously*. Faith is dangerous and costly. Faith is also incredibly inspiring.

What would your church do in those circumstances? What should it do? Are there other areas in your community that are in desperate need for the church to take action? Are you willing to commit to the task at hand, no matter the cost?

84

LOVE FOR ONE ANOTHER COMES FROM GOD

*If you should not love yourself even for your own sake,
but for the sake of the One who is the most worthy of your
love, no one has a right to be angry if you also love them
for God's sake. For this is the divinely established law of
love: "Love your neighbor as yourself." But also, "Love the
Lord your God with all your heart and with all your soul
and with all your mind." And so you should devote all
your thoughts, your whole life, and your whole intelligence
to the One who gave you these things in the first place.*

On Christian Teaching, 1.22.21, trans. J. Shaw*.

We should love people for who they are. And truly we could all benefit from acceptance without judgment. The trouble is, we aren't very good at loving ourselves or each other. Self-centeredness is just as much a problem as low self-esteem.

As Augustine points out, Jesus tells us we must love God first. Loving ourselves and each other comes second. Why is this? Because God is the source of love itself. And while we might think loving God means loving everyone else less, the opposite is true. When we love God with all our hearts, souls, and minds—as Jesus commands us—we love ourselves and others more fully, more deeply. We love them as they are supposed to be loved.

Love begins and ends with God.

Bring to mind, then, the people in your life who are a source of frustration—or worse. Bring to mind, also, those you love and care for. Pray God will allow you to love both—not for their sake but for His.

And what about the conflicted feelings you have about yourself? Pray for God to transform your ideas about self-love. May they be formed in His image and not shaped to fit your own.

85

A LOVE POEM TO GOD

Late did I love You, beauty so old, and so new;
Late did I love You. And see, You were within,
and I was without, and looked for You there.
Misshapen, I rushed among the beautiful things You had made,
You were with me, but I was not with You.
Those things kept me far from You—
which, unless they were in You, would not be.
You called, and cried aloud, and forced open my deafness;
You blazed and shone, and chased away my blindness;
You were fragrant, and I drew in my
breath and panted after You.
I tasted, and now hunger and thirst for more.
You touched me, and I burned for Your peace.

Confessions, 10.27.38, trans. J. G. Pilkington*.

I invite you to read the poem aloud. Augustine wrote this so it would be spoken. The poem is the cry of a heart—a heart that finally found its home. A heart that finally found true love.

Read it again. As you listen, consider the passion and the desire. People don't normally talk about God like this. Others don't normally talk *to* God like this. Doing so may make you uncomfortable. But why? Do you know God actually loves you *this much*?

Read it a third time. God is with you. Even as you seek Him, He is already here. And whatever it is you know, there is more to be known. Whatever it is you love, there is more to be loved.

Do you long to be overcome by God's presence? Do you want to know His love for you so deeply that it is overwhelming? You are *so* loved. You have nothing to fear.

A NEW SONG

"Sing to Him a new song." Cast off the old! You know the new song . . . it does not belong to "the old." Only the new people know how it goes—those whom grace has restored from out of their old selves, those who now belong to the new covenant, the kingdom of heaven. All our love sighs and sings a new song to Him. So let us sing a new song, not with words, but with our lives.

EXPOSITIONS ON THE PSALMS, 32.8, TRANS. S. WATTS.

L ife can get old, even for the relatively young. Past hurts and regrets can build up; present cares and anxieties can weigh us down. Stuck in a draining and monotonous pattern, each day can seem little different from the last. Some of us feel this way from time to time. Others feel this way most of the time. But we all know, somewhere deep in our hearts, life is not supposed to be like this. We long for something new.

When Augustine tells us to sing a new song, he doesn't mean we should be blindly optimistic or "fake it till we make it." He wants us to live lives of praise, lives full of gratitude. If we find that difficult, it might be that although we've been offered new life, we still cling to the old.

For the old self considers its place in the world; but the new self seeks the kingdom of heaven. And the old self groans under the weight of sin; but the new self is lifted by God's love.

I invite you, then, to make a list. Write down all you are thankful for, even if you may not feel like it at the moment. What has God renewed in your life? What has He told you to leave in the past? May God open your eyes and your heart to all He has done. Practice praise, and your life will resound with a new song—a song of resurrected life!

87

TO KNOW GOD TRULY

Let me know You, You who know me; let me know You, as I am known. Strength of my soul, enter into it, and prepare it for Yourself that You may have and hold it "without stain or wrinkle." This is my hope, which is why "I have spoken," and I rejoice in this hope, when I rejoice as I should.

CONFESSIONS, 10.1.1, TRANS. J. G. PILKINGTON*.

T he end of a truly great concert finally arrives. The performer comes to the microphone one last time before exiting the stage. *I love you all so much.* The audience cheers and roars its approval. The feeling is mutual. It was a wonderful evening, well worth every dollar.

Now, the audience knows the artist doesn't *truly* love each spectator. And the audience, as much as it loves the person performing, doesn't really know the artist either. But it feels good to say and hear it anyway.

If we are honest with ourselves, we probably think of God's love in a similar way at times. Sure, He loves us. But He doesn't *really* know us, right? With a whole universe to look after, is He really all that interested in knowing us?

For Augustine, however, the answer to that question is a resounding *yes*. You are known and you are loved, *so much more* than you can possibly imagine. But it isn't a one-way street. Unlike the performer on the stage, you can also actually know God, as unbelievable as that might sound.

Knowing God involves learning about Him, but it isn't limited to that. Knowing God means having Him transform and purify you. It means learning to love through the One who is love.

What an amazing thing it is to know God and to be known by God! Do you want to know Him? Ask Him to reveal Himself to you. Do you want to know yourself as He knows you? Ask that you will see yourself as He sees you. You are known and you are loved. And you will never be the same.

WHAT IS PRAYER?

I have already said it, and will say it again, I do this for the love of Your love. For as we pray, the Truth says, "Your Father knows what you need before you ask Him." We show You our love as we confess to You our own miseries and Your mercies upon us. We do this so You may free us completely, so we may cease to be wretched in ourselves, and be happy in You.

CONFESSIONS, 11.1.1, TRANS. J. G. PILKINGTON*.

W hen you think of prayer, what comes to mind?

For many, prayer probably means asking for something. We have a need, and we ask God to meet it. It is usually a one-sided conversation. We don't expect God to answer in word but in deed. On many occasions in the Bible, however, God started the conversation and back-and-forth dialogue took place. But we rarely think this happens today.

Jesus tells us, however, that God knows what we want before we ask Him (Matthew 6:8). So what is the point of asking in the first place? Why pray at all?

Augustine tells us prayer is not really about asking for something. Prayer is about loving someone. Prayer is about loving God.

When we ask for help, when we lay our burdens down before Him, when we confess our sins to Him—we cast aside our self-reliance. We put ourselves at the mercy of our loving Creator. Like the prodigal son, our prayer brings us home into the arms of our Father, who is already running to meet us and embrace us (Luke 15:20).

When you pray, by all means ask God to meet your needs. But do not expect a one-sided conversation. Listen intently. You may be surprised by what you hear. Remember too, the very act of prayer is an act of love. Much like having a conversation with a significant other, a family member, or a friend—it may not even matter what you talk about. Just pray.

89

SEEING GOD FACE-TO-FACE

*For as "we walk by faith, not by sight," we certainly do not yet
see God . . . "face-to-face." . . . But before we have the ability
to see and to perceive God—as He can be seen and perceived,
which is permitted to the pure in heart, for "blessed are the
pure in heart, for they shall see God"—He must be loved by
faith. Otherwise, it will not be possible for the heart to be
cleansed, in order that it may be ready and suitable to see Him.*

ON THE TRINITY, 8.4.6, TRANS. A. W. HADDAN*.

S eeing is believing. Or so it is said. Yet millions upon millions believe in what they cannot see. But do we believe in order that we *will* see? As the apostle Paul says, do we believe in expectation that one day we will actually see our Maker face-to-face (1 Corinthians 13:12)?

In the Bible, God told Moses that Moses could not see His face and live. But He allowed Moses to catch a glimpse as He passed by. The face of Moses then shone so brightly that his appearance terrified the other Israelites. He had to wear a veil until it faded (Exodus 34:29–35).

Augustine knew something of the awesome power of God. He also knew he was in no state to see Him. In the same way that flawed pottery is destroyed by the intense heat of the kiln, he knew he was still too broken and too sinful to survive in God's presence. But he loved his Creator. He desired to see Him and be with Him. So Augustine loved by faith. And through that faith, he knew God would purify him.

This is not purity for its own sake. This is a purity that exists at the very heart of Love—the very heart of God.

Imagine you will soon see God face-to-face. What do you expect to see? Will it bring you joy or fear? Do you have unfinished business to attend to?

Will you say this prayer? "Lord, purify my heart. Grow my faith in Your love. I want to see You for all that You are."

90

SEEK HIM, FIND
HIM, PRAISE HIM

*And those who seek the Lord shall praise Him. For those who
seek shall find Him, and those who find Him shall praise Him.
Let me seek You, Lord, in calling on You, and call on You in
believing in You; for You have been preached to us. O Lord,
my faith calls on You—that faith which You have given to
me, which You have breathed into me through the incarnation
of your Son, through the ministry of Your Preacher.*

CONFESSIONS, 1.1.1, TRANS. J. G. PILKINGTON*.

S eek the Lord. Whom else should you search for? Who else is worthier of this pursuit? Could anyone or anything be more important? The universe is in His hands. The very beat of your heart obeys Him. You ought to seek Him with your whole heart.

Find the Lord. If you seek Him, you will find Him. He will reveal Himself to you. And in revealing Himself, He will transform you into His likeness. And then *you* will truly be found.

Praise the Lord. When you find Him, you can do nothing else. For what amount of gratitude could you possibly express to your Creator—for your life, for His love? Everything is a gift, lovingly and graciously given.

Hear Augustine when he speaks. You cannot earn God's love. You cannot find God in your own strength. You received your faith freely so you can freely give yourself to Him.

God makes a way. His Spirit preaches to your heart and encourages you along. His Son breathes new life into your soul and guides you on your journey.

Seek Him. Find Him. Praise Him. It is who you are meant to be.

BIBLIOGRAPHY

Translations and modifications by the writer and compiler of this volume have been marked using an * if modified. Both translations and modifications use the Latin texts from the *Patrologia Latina* series, which have been digitally reproduced at https://www.augustinus.it/latino/index.htm.

Augustine. *City of God*. Translated by Marcus Dods. Nicene and Post-Nicene Fathers, First Series, Vol. 2. Buffalo, NY: Christian Literature Publishing Co., 1887.

———. *Confessions*. Translated by J. G. Pilkington. Nicene and Post-Nicene Fathers, First Series, Vol. 1. Buffalo, NY: Christian Literature Publishing Co., 1887.

———. *Confessions and Enchiridion*. Translated by Albert C. Outler. Philadelphia, PA: Westminster Press, 1955.

———. *Expositions on the Psalms*. Translated by J. E. Tweed. Nicene and Post-Nicene Fathers, First Series, Vol. 8. Buffalo, NY: Christian Literature Publishing Co., 1888.

———. *Letters*. Translated by J. G. Cunningham. Nicene and Post-Nicene Fathers, First Series, Vol. 1. Buffalo, NY: Christian Literature Publishing Co., 1887.

———. *On the Catechizing of the Uninstructed.* Translated by S. D. F. Salmond. Nicene and Post-Nicene Fathers, First Series, Vol. 3. Buffalo, NY: Christian Literature Publishing Co., 1887.

———. *On Christian Teaching.* Translated by James Shaw. Nicene and Post-Nicene Fathers, First Series, Vol. 2. Buffalo, NY: Christian Literature Publishing Co., 1887.

———. *On the Gift of Perseverance.* Translated by Peter Holmes and Robert Ernest Wallis. Nicene and Post-Nicene Fathers, First Series, Vol. 5. Buffalo, NY: Christian Literature Publishing Co., 1887.

———. *On Nature and Grace.* Translated by Peter Holmes and Robert Ernest Wallis. Nicene and Post-Nicene Fathers, First Series, Vol. 5. Buffalo, NY: Christian Literature Publishing Co., 1887.

———. *Sermons.* Translated by R. G. MacMullen. Nicene and Post-Nicene Fathers, First Series, Vol. 6. Buffalo, NY: Christian Literature Publishing Co., 1888.

———. *Tractates on the Gospel of John.* Translated by John Gibb. Nicene and Post-Nicene Fathers, First Series, Vol. 7. Buffalo, NY: Christian Literature Publishing Co., 1888.

———. *The Trinity.* Translated by Arthur West Haddan. Nicene and Post-Nicene Fathers, First Series, Vol. 3. Buffalo, NY: Christian Literature Publishing Co., 1887.